WILDFLOWERS

OF INDIANA WOODLANDS

by
Sylvan T. Runkel and Alvin F. Bull

ISBN: 0-87069-311-5

Wallace Homestead Book Co.
1912 Grand Ave.
Des Moines, Iowa 50305

About this book. . .

This book was designed to help the casual observer become better acquainted with the more interesting wildflowers of the state's woodlands.

Common names for a species often vary widely from area to area. Those in frequent use are listed. A locality may use still others.

A common name may be applied to more than one species. So botannical names are included for precise identification. Although knowledge of this two-name system is not necessary for enjoying the natural beauty of wildflowers, the system is both practical and useful. The genus names applies to a group of closely related plants and the species name to individual kinds of plants with in the genus. Family names are still broader groupings of related genera. In a few cases, botanists disagree on names - usually in honest dispute over how far to subdivide a genus into different species. In most of these cases, we followed one of the leading state authorities and noted the area of disagreement.

The genus and species names, usually from Latin or Greek, are often descriptive of the plant. The meaning, and sometimes the probable origin, of genus and species names is listed as an item of interest.

For each flower, a section on where the species is found will help both with identification and with a search for that particular species.

Descriptions of plants and flowers are as accurate as we can make them in nontechnical terms. Of course, nature does not make all plants of single species uniform - nor even all flowers of a single plant the same size and shade of color.

Species are listed in approximate order of flowering time under normal conditions. But time of blooming may vary considerably with weather, soil and other environmental factors – plants try to blossom and produce seed for reproduction even under harshest of conditions. So our listing serves only as a useful guide to time of flowering, especially in relation to other species.

Some of the species included are as much at home in the prairie as in the woodlands. Some may be regarded more as weeds than as flowers. Poison ivy, poison sunac, stinging nettle, and some sticky-seeded species are included to help flower lovers recognize them and give them respectful distance.

Mostly, the authors hope the emphasis on pictures and interesting information about each species will increase enjoyment from visits to the woodlands. Especially, we hope teachers will find our approach useful in increasing the interest of students and the amount of information they retain. To this end, information on how Indians and pioneers made use of individual species is a regular part of the text. Note that the spelling of Indian names is as we found them recorded by early botanists, physicians, and herblists.

Early medicinal uses of our woodland plants form a basis for much of modern medicine. A few plants still provide the active ingredients of prescription medicines. More often, nature's chemicals have been synthesized in the laboratory for added purity and closer control of dosage. A few plants - some in this book - are still under active investigation with promise for treating modern maladies such as cancer.

In many cases however, any benefit from some of the early uses must have been purely psychological. Indeed, some may well have done more harm than good. The trial and error basis of early medicine must have included many disastrous results.

It is often difficult to tell whether uses originated with Indians or with early settlers. There were no written records until the settlers came. Exchange of information between pioneers and friendly Indians was a frequent occurrence.

Most common method of preparing early plant "medicines" was a decoction. The desired parts of plants were gathered in advance, dried for storage, and boiled in water as needed to produce the decoction or "tea".

CONSERVATION: An increasing number of the more delicate wildflower species are threatened with extinction as their habitat is modified. Pasturing of woodlands, clearing trees and brush, draining of wet areas, and many other of man's actions may make an area no longer suitable for some species of wildflowers.

Fortunately, a few areas are being set aside as preserves by concerned individuals, government agencies, and conservation groups. The reader's help and cooperation can aid in expanding such efforts.

Wildflowers, as well as their habitats, tend to be fragile. In general, they are seldom suited for bouquets. They are better left growing as nature intended - and preserved by memory or photograph.

For those who would like to try raising wildflowers in their yards or gardens, obtaining stock or seeds from a nursery specializing in wildflowers is the preferred approach. Transplanting from natural woodlands has less chance of success and is to be recommended only where plants are in danger of immediate destruction.

ACKNOWLEDGMENTS: Cooperation, encouragement and other assistance of many people – both professional and dedicated amateurs in the fields of botany, photography, and wild flower observation – have made this book possible. We take this means of expressing our sincere gratitude.

Some have contributed so extensively of their time and expertise that we must publicly acknowledge our debt to them. They include Dr. Myrle Burk, retired; Dr. Robert Drexler of Coe College; Jane B. Eddy of the Des Moines Founders Garden Club; Dr. Lawrence J. Eilers of University of Northern Iowa; Dr. Benjamin F. Graham, Jr., of Grinnell College; Dr. J. F. Hennen of Purdue University; Dr. Roger Q. Landers of Iowa State University; Dr. Robert H. Mohlenbrock of Southern Illinois University; Dean Roosa, ecologist for the Iowa Preserves Board; and Ray Schulenberg of Morton Arboretum.

Much of the typing was done with skill and patience by Mary Frances Dwyer.

What would have been a long and tedious task of preparing the index was made easy by the generous assistance of Mr. and Mrs. LeRoy G. Pratt.

To these people, we offer a special thanks.

DEDICATION: To our wives, who helped with research, proofreading, editing, and overall design of this book and who provided the unending encouragement to help us complete the task, we gratefully dedicate this book.

Sylvan T. Runkel
Alvin F. Bull

CONTENTS

About the authors . . .

SYLVAN T. RUNKEL, best known as "Sy", is widely respected for his special ability to communicate with young people as well as adults in a warm and sensitive manner. He has helped plan conservation education programs, develop outdoor classrooms, and lay out nature trails.

Although retired, he is much in demand for programs on natural resources and for work with conservation groups. Among other activities, he has been president of the Iowa chapters of the Soil Conservation Society of America, the American Foresters, and the Wildlife Society. As chairman of the Nature Preserves Board and a board member of Nature Conservancy, he has been instrumental in preserving many important natural areas for future generations.

His awards and honors are numerous – including Iowa Conservationist of the year, Federal Civil Servant of the year, Iowa Conservation Hall of Fame, Nature Conservancy's Oak Leaf Award, Frudden Award of the Iowa Chapter of American Foresters, fellow of the Iowa Academy of Science, and fellow of the Soil Conservation Society of America.

Except for 5 years as a glider pilot in World War II, the thrust of his 40 years with the federal government (mostly Soil Conservation Service) was conservation.

He and his wife Bernie live in Des Moines, Iowa.

ALVIN F. (AL) BULL is vice president of Farm Progress Companies and editorial director for *Indiana Prairie Farmer, Prairie Farmer, Wallaces Farmer,* and *Wisconsin Agriculturist* magazines.

His concern for young people and the environment we provide for them led to participation in education and conservation groups and included serving as temporary editor followed by several years as chairman of the editorial board of the *Journal of Soil and Water Conservation.*

He has served as president of the Iowa Chapter of the Soil Conservation Society of America, chairman of the National Farm Institute, and president of the American Agricultural Editors Association. He has been a member of the Governor's Committee on Conservation of Outdoor Resources, the Governor's Educational Advisory Committee, the committee to develop an environmental education plan for Iowa, the Title III – ESEA (innovation in education) advisory committee.

His honors and awards include president's citation and fellow of the Soil Conservation Society of America, leadership award from the Iowa Soil Committee, Honorary Master Farmer, and several journalism awards.

He and his wife Carol live in Glen Ellyn, Illinois.

WILDFLOWERS
OF INDIANA WOODLANDS

by
Sylvan T. Runkel and Alvin F. Bull

Skunk cabbage: *Symplocarpus foetidus* (L.) Nutt.

Other common names: collard, meadow cabbage, pole cat weed, pole weed, skunk weed, swamp cabbage.

Symplocarpus: from Greek meaning "connected fruits", from the way its fruits are connected together.

Foetidus: from Latin meaning "foul-smelling", characteristic of the plant when any part is crushed.

Calla family: *Araceae (formerly Arum).*

Found on humus-rich soils of wet woodlands and marshes in the eastern part of the state. Blooms mid-February to April.

One of the earliest plants, skunk cabbage often appears before the snow is gone. Leaves emerge after the spathe, persist into September, and then quickly decay. They are massive heart-shapes, and may be more than 2 feet long and nearly as wide. Their smooth margins and thick pale ribs remind one of cabbage leaves. Several leaves, usually six to eight per plant, stand in a tight cluster beside the spathe. The long peioles have deep grooves on the upper side.

The perennial root system consists of a large upright rhizome with numerous rootlets.

The fleshy spathe, a distinctive mottled brown and yellow-green, emerges tightly closed. A slit-like opening widens to give a sea shell shape perhaps 6 inches high and half as wide. Within the spathe stands a knobby inch-high spadix covered with bright yellow anthers of the tiny flowers.

It enlarges to a spongy mass with individual fruits just beneath the surface. As the spadix decays, it leaves a pile of pebble-like seeds on the soil surface. Flies and other insects attracted by the foetid odor or the warmth provide pollination.

As rapid cellular expansion begins in the flowers, accelerated respiration maintains more or less constant temperature in surrounding plant tissues for as long as 2 weeks – as much as 30 degrees celsius above ambient air temerature even when air temperatures drop as low as – 14 degrees celsius. By some still unknown mechanism, respiration rate increases as air temperature decreases. Others of the *Araceae* family produce similar heat but for only a few hours and not at such low temperatures.

Roots and young leaves of skunk cabbage served as food for Iroquois, Seneca, and probably other tribes. Drying and/or thorough cooking decreases a concentration of calcium oxalate. Careful identification was necessary to avoid confusion with the poisonous Indian poke, *Veratum viride* Ait., which somewhat resembles skunk cabbage and may be known by that name.

The Meskwaki tribe applied rootlets to ease toothache. They also used crushed leaf petioles as a wet dressing for severe bruises. The Menomini tribe used a tea of the rootlets to stop external bleeding. Winnebago and Dakota tribes used the plant to treat asthma. One tribe inhaled the sharp odor of crushed leaves as a treatment for headache.

Until late in the 19th century, pioneers used skunk cabbage to treat respiratory problems, rheumatism, dropsy, ringworm, skin sores, muscle spasms, and other disorders.

. . . photograph by Randall A. Maas

Trillium: *Trillium* many species

Other common names: birthroot, toad shade, wake robin – and many others, often applying to a single species.

Trillium: from Latin *tres* meaning "three" and *lilium* for lily. Both leaves and petals occur in units of three.

Species: Several species are found in the state.

Lily family: *Liliaceae.*

Found throughout the state usually in rich moist woodlands where soils are deep and loose. Most trilliums flower early, starting in March, but some bloom as late as June.

Plants and flowers of this genus have distinctly related characteristics. A single smooth erect stem arises from a perennial bulb. Toward the top of the stem is a whorl of three leaves with net veining and smooth margins. A single showy flower with three petals tops the stem.

The following are among the trilliums found in the state:

Little snow trillium, *T. nivale* Riddell (snowy): grows 2 to 6 inches tall. White flower. Blooms March to May. Locally called dwarf white or snow trillium.

Toadshade, *T. sessile* L. (without leaf petioles): grows 4 to 12 inches tall. Flower is dark red, purple, or greenish yellow. Leaves and flowers without petioles. Leaves are usually mottled with brownish coloring.

Prairie trillium, *T. recurvatum* Beck (recurved): grows 6 to 18 inches tall. Flowers red-brown, maroon, purplish, or greenish yellow. Similar to toadshade except leaves have petioles and sepals are curved back (recurved). Found in woodlands despite the common name.

Large white trillium, *T. grandiflorum* (Michx.) Salisb. (large flowered): grows 8 to 16 inches tall. Each petal up to 2 inches long and with wavy margins. Usually white, sometimes pink or greenish. Flowers usually on long erect stem.

Nodding trillium, *T. cernuum* L. (nodding): grows 6 to 24 inches tall. White flower with petals to one inch long. Flower stalk curves downward so flower droops or nods below the leaves. Leaves have short petioles.

White wakerobin, *T. flexipes* Raf. (with bent flower-stalk): resembles nodding trillium except that leaves have no petioles.

Birthroot was a name given to trilliums by pioneers who understood that Indians used the plant to induce labor and for other childbirth problems. This has not been verified.

Astringent and antiseptic qualities of the root led to extensive use by various Indian tribes for treating open wounds and sores – even for internal bleeding. The Menomini Indians made a wet dressing of freshly dug roots for eye inflamation. The Potawatomi steeped powdered roots in water to produce a wash for sore nipples. The Chippewas scraped the second layer of "bark" from the roots. Steeped in water, this was used as ear drops. They sometimes treated rheumatism by "injecting" a tea of powdered roots into the affected area. This was done by pounding the area with a special tool – several needles fastened to the end of a stick.   *...photo by LeRoy G. Pratt*

Hepatica: *Hepatica americana*, (DC.) Ker.

Other common names: golden trefoil, herb trinity, ivy flower, liverleaf, liverwort, mouse ear, squirrel cup.

Hepatica: from Latin *epatikos* meaning "affecting the liver", probably from the color and shape of the dead leaves.

Americana: meaning "American", indicating that it was first found on this continent. Another species *H. acutiloba* D. C. (from Latin meaning "sharp lobe", describing the pointed leaf shape) is also found in the state.

Buttercup family: *Ranunculaceae.*

Found throughout the state, usually on medium dry leaf-covered soils of wooded uplands. The round-lobed species prefers neutral to acid soils, while the sharp-lobed species prefers alkaline or high lime soils. Flowering time is March to June.

Leaves arise on slender hairy petioles from a common point at about ground level to a height of a few inches. They have three lobes, rounded in the case of *H. americana* DC. Ker. and usually broader than long. Lobes of *H. acutiloba* DC. are more pointed, longer than broad. The leaves, to 3 inches across, are light green and hairy when young, turning dark olive green when older. They persist through the winter becoming purplish or liver-colored.

The perennial roots are fibrous and profusely branched.

Individual flowers occur at the top of individual hairy stalks about 6 inches high. What appear to be 6 to 10 white to pink or bluish purple petals are actually colored sepals. The flowers, which appear before the new leaves, are about an inch across.

Just below each flower is a whorl of three small unlobed leaves which could easily be mistaken for sepals. But close examination reveals a short length of stem between the flower and the leaves.

In the Middle Ages, a widespread belief held that if a plant in some way resembled an organ of the human body, that plant would be useful in treating disorders of that organ. This belief, mistaken though it was, is known as the "doctrine of signatures." Since hepatica leaves somewhat resemble the shape and color of the liver, it was once used for liver ailments. In later years, the hepaticas were considered of little or no medicinal value, but leaves were sometimes collected as a source of tannin.

It has mildly astringent properties, probably due to tannin in mature leaves. It has been used to treat cough, lung ailments, indigestion, liver ailments, and even hemorrhoids.

Indians found other medicinal uses. Chippewas made a tea of powdered roots to be taken internally by children with convulsions.

A Meskwaki medicine man described use of hepatica in these words: "when the mouth gets twisted and the eyes get crossed, this root is brewed into a tea and the face is washed until it returns to normal."

...photograph by Elvin Warrick
courtesy of Illinois Natural History Survey

Bloodroot: *Sanguinaria canadensis* L.

Other common names: corn root, pain ease, red Indian paint, red puccoon, red root, snake bite, sweet slumber, tetterwort, tumeric, white puccoon.

Sanguinaria: from Latin *sanguinarius* meaning "bleeding" – referring to the bright red juice which oozes from a cut or broken root.

Canadensis: meaning "of Canada."

Poppy family: *Papaveraceae*.

Found in rich moist but well-drained woodlands throughout the state – usually in small colonies of plants. Blooms March through May.

This erect but low-growing perennial makes most of its growth early before the forest floor is shaded by the foliage of the trees. It grows 6 to 14 inches high from a slightly branching horizontal rootstock. The thick, to one inch in diameter, salmon-colored rootstock oozes a bright red juice when cut or broken. This red juice rapidly coagulates to protect the wounded area.

A light green leaf, paler underneath, emerges from the ground closely coiled around the flower stalk. After the flower appears, the leaf unfurls to full width – perhaps as much as one foot across. It is broadly circular with numerous lobes. Basal lobes are usually larger and more rounded than the others. Margins of the lobes have coarse rounded teeth.

The single white flower commonly has eight petals, rarely as many as 16. Larger petals alternate with slightly smaller ones producing a somewhat squarish outline perhaps an inch and a half across. The flower is borne on its own stalk which is taller than the leaves. A close look shows varying shades of white within each petal making an intricate design.

The root is poisonous. Like other members of the poppy family, it contains alkaloids closely related to morphine. Chippewas drank a tea of the roots to relieve stomach cramps. The Menomeni and Potwatomi tribes used a similar tea to bathe burns. At times, they chewed the root and used the spittle on burns. Some New England Indians and early settlers squeezed juice from the root onto a lump of maple sugar and held it in the mouth to cure sore throat. Any internal use was a dangerous practice in view of the poisonous characteristic of the roots. Bloodroot was also used externally on warts, ringworms, fungus infections, chronic eczema, and cancerous growths.

In early medical practice, bloodroot was sometimes used to treat asthma, bronchitis, and various heart ailments.

Indians also used the red juice of the roots as a dye for fabrics, tools, and warpaint. Captain John Smith reported that the Indian women chosen by Chief Powhatan to be his companions painted their bodies with bloodroot. Early settlers also used bloodroot as a dyestuff. Adding oak bark provided tannin which helped set the color and make it more permanent.

. . . photograph by W. K. Hollingsworth

Rue anemone: *Anemonella thalictroides* (L.) Spach.

Other common names: anemone.

*Anemonella:*a diminutive of *Anemone,* as this plant has sometimes been called. The word *Anemone* is a corruption of an ancient Greek and Latin name for the mythological Adonis from whose blood spilled upon the ground the crimson-flowered anemone of the Orient is said to have sprung.

Thalictroides: for "like *Thalictrum*", the meadow rue, which has similar leaves. This is the only species in the genus *Anemonella.*

Buttercup family: *Ranunculaceae.*

Found throughout the state in dry open woodlands, especially on slopes. Blooms late in March to June.

The leaf structure of rue anemone is botanically complex. What seem to be six leaves in a whorl just below the flowers are actually two bracts on the flower stalk. Each bract has three segments on individual stems. The flower stalks are usually less than 9 inches tall. Two basal leaves appear after flowering. Each of these has three leaflets which are similar in appearance to the bract leaflets. The basal leaves have long petioles. The total bract has no petiole, but leaflets of the bract may have stems of their own.

The leaflets of both the bracts and the true leaves are smooth, thin and pale green. They are generally rounded with three rounded lobes toward the tip. The shallow notch between lobes is in contrast to the deep notches of false rue anemone.

Individual leaflets may be as much as three-fourths inch across.

A cluster of thickened tuberous roots gives this perennial its rapid start in early spring.

The flowers are borne on slender individual stalks originating at the point where the bracts attach to the stem. Usually there are two or three, sometimes more, flowers in each cluster. The flowers have five to 10 petal-like sepals, no true petals. The color is usually whitish, sometimes shading to a magenta pink. The oval "petals" form a shallow saucer, perhaps three-fourths inch across, with numerous yellow-green stamens in the center. The rue anemone flowers are long-lasting compared to most other early spring flowers. They may be difficult to distinguish from flowers of the false rue anemone, which tends to blossom somewhat earlier. They are also similar to flowers of the woodland anemone, *Anemone quinquefolia* L., which has but a single flower on each stem.

Occasionally "double" flowers will be found in the wild. A double-flowered variety has been developed for use in gardens.

No medicinal uses of rue anemone by Indians or pioneers are known. But the clusters of tubers have been harvested for food by both Indians and pioneers. In some Pennsylvania mountain areas, the tubers earned the name "wild potatoe."

This delicate little plant is becoming uncommon and deserves protection if it is to be preserved. Despite the tuberous roots, this species is easily harmed by division of its root system. So it is difficult to transplant and should be left undisturbed in its natural habitat.   ...*photograph by LeRoy G. Pratt*

Toothwort: *Dentaria laciniata* Muhl.

Other common names: crinkle root, cut-leafed toothwort, milkmaids, pepper root, pepper wort, spring blossoms.

Dentaria: from Latin *dens* for "tooth", perhaps describing the slightly closed flowers, the sharply-toothed leaves, or the tubers on the roots.

Laciniata: from Latin for "torn", describing the somewhat ragged appearance of the leaves. Another species, *D. diphylla* Michx., with only two leaves on the stem is found in our area.

Mustard family: *Brassicaceae (Cruciferae. This old family name is from Latin meaning "cross bearer" for the four petals of the flower which form a cross.)*

Found throughout the state, often is large patches, on rich soils of medium to moist shady woodlands. Blooms March to May.

Leaves of toothwort are of two types. One group appears as a whorl, usually of three leaves, below the flowers on the flower stem. The other group is basal leaves on long petioles which develop from the crown after flowering. Both sets of leaves look much alike – as much as 5 inches across and deeply cut into three segments. The two outer segments may also be so deeply cut as to give the appearance of five separate segments. Each segment is also deeply cut or coarsely toothed. *Dentaria* species may hybridize and produce variations in plant types.

The deep perennial root system is a necklace of small white (or yellow-brown) tubers connected by slender roots. Individual tubers are from one half to 2 inches long.

The erect flowering stem grows to 15 inches tall. Flowers, usually no more than six, grow in a loose terminal cluster. Individual flowers, to three-fourths inch across, have four white petals which take on a pinkish cast as they get older. The petals curve outward forming a cross and curve slightly backward at their tips.

The slender fruit capsules, to 1½ inches long, curve upward.

Pioneers gathered the little tubers in the early spring and used them throughout the year for seasoning soups, stews, meats, and other dishes. Eaten raw, the little tubers have the flavor of a radish or a mild horseradish. Stored tubers wrinkle like a prune as they dry out. This characteristic gave rise to the name crinkle root. The name toothwort may come from the tooth-like shape of the fleshy tubers. As long as only the outer end of the tuber system away from the growing stem was harvested, the plant was not seriously harmed.

No uses by Indians are known but they probably learned of food uses from the pioneers if they lacked prior knowledge. Exchange of information about food and medicinal use of plants was common on the frontier where food was often scarce and doctors were seldom to be found.

. . . photograph by William Beecher
courtesy of Chicago Academy of Science

Spring beauty: *Claytonia virginica* L.

Other common names: fairy spuds, good morning spring, ground nut, mayflower, wild potato.

Claytonia: in honor of John Clayton, early American botanist and physician.

Virginica: meaning "of Virginia", probably for the location in which it was studied and given its first scientific name.

Purslane family: *Portulacaceae.*

Found throughout the state on rich soils of moist open woodlands. Plants may be scattered but often occur in patches. Blooms March into May.

The pinkish weak watery stem is usually about 6 inches tall at flowering. It continues to grow to perhaps one foot by the time seeds mature. The plant disappears in late June.

Two opposite leaves – long, tapering, narrow, smooth and somewhat thickened – occur about halfway up the stem. A third and larger leaf, usually 3 to 7 inches long and no more than a half inch wide, is often present at the base of the stem. The plant parts are fragile and easily broken.

The perennial root system is a dark-colored tuber that is mostly less than an inch across. Bundles of fibrous rootlets branch from the tuber. Though the plant has disappeared by late June, the tubers lie dormant deep in the soil awaiting an early start the following spring.

Small delicate flowers, usually less than a half inch across, vary from white to pink with characteristic darker pink veining.

The flowers are arranged in two rows along one side of the main stem. The flowers themselves turn toward the sunshine. Each has its own short slender flower stalk. These stalks droop before the petals open, straighten upon blooming, and droop again as the flower withers and the seed forms. Usually only one or two flowers are open at one time. Each flower has five rounded petals and only two green sepals. The flowers prefer light and close up at night and during cloudy weather.

The fruit is a short three-valved capsule containing several tiny black shiny seeds. At times, seeds may be expelled with sufficient force to carry them several inches from the parent plant.

Both Indians and early pioneers dug the roundish perennial tubers for food. These starchy bulbs were eaten raw or boiled as a potato substitute. Their flavor is bland, often described as resembling chestnuts.

Leaves were nibbled fresh, added to salads, or used as greens.

This plant and its close relatives provide feed for wildlife. Rodents, and in other parts of the country even the ferocious grizzly, dig and eat the tubers. Moose, deer, and elk browse on the above-ground parts in early spring.

This species is delicate and digging the bulbs or persistent picking of the flowers will destroy the plants. The flowers wilt quickly and are not suitable for bouquets.

. . . photograph by Charles J. Hoffman

Virginia bluebells: *Mertensia virginica* (L.) DC.

Other common names: tree lungwort, Virginia cowslip.

Mertensia: in honor of an early German botanist, Franz Karl Mertens.

Virginica: meaing "of Virginia", referring to the first detailed description made from a specimen collected in Virginia.

Forget-me-not family: *Boraginaceae (Borage).*

 Found throughout the state on rich moist soils of woodlands, usually bottomlands. Blooms March through May.

 The pale fleshy stem grows erect to 2 feet tall. It is weak and watery – quite fragile. It may be covered with soft hairs, more often smooth. The stem may be branched or simple.

 The leaves are alternate along the stem. They are smooth pale blue-green ovals as much as 5 inches long and 1½ inches wide. Leaf margins are smooth. Prominent veins join inside the leaf margins. Lower leaves have short petioles, but upper leaves may have none. Petioles have distinct "wings" or margins.

 The gnarled black-coated perennial roots are tuberous and extend deep into the soil.

 The plant has a short season. A forest floor carpeted with colorful bluebells in early spring may show no trace of the plants by midsummer. Stinging nettles and jewelweeds are the likely successors.

 Loose clusters of tubular pink buds open into trumpet-shaped flowers of crisp porcelain blue. Each flower, three-fourths to one inch long, nods on its own slender stalk. The flare of the bells is five-pleated, sometimes with shallow lobes.

 Bees sometimes perforate the tube rather than obtain nectar in the usual manner. The drooping habit of the flowers and the length of the tube probably made it difficult for bees to reach the nectar otherwise.

 Fruits are wrinkled rounded nutlets about one-eight of an inch across. Four fruits are produced by each flower.

 The name lungwort was applied by pioneers because the plant resembled one in Europe which has whitish spots on the leaves. The European species was once thought to be a cure for lung disorders. Some pioneers tried Virginia bluebells for this purpose but without success. It has also been considered to provide a general tonic for improving health of persons who were feeling poorly but without specific complaints.

 Other uses by Indians and pioneers for food or medicinal purposes are not known but Virginia bluebells have been, and still are used in flower gardens. Seeds can be planted soon after they are ripe. *...photograph by James P. Rowan*

Spring cress: *Cardamine bulbosa* (Schreb.) BSP.

Other common names: cardamine.

Cardamine: from early Greek word *kardamon* used by Dioscorides for some cress, perhaps because some members of this genus were thought at that time to be useful for treating heart ailments.

Bulbosa: from Latin meaning generally "having a bulb type root system."

Mustard family: *Brassicaceae (Cruciferae).*

Found throughout the state around springs and in wet bottomland woods or meadows. Blooms March into June.

A smooth slender stem grows upright, usually less than 2 feet tall. The upper stem is sometimes branched. Scattered leaves are alternate along the stem. The stem leaves have a few coarse teeth and vary from rounded oval to lance shaped. The lower ones are more rounded and have short petioles. The upper leaves are more pointed, without petioles, and may be as much as 2 inches long.

Basal leaves arising from ground level are rounded to heart-shaped, usually as much as an inch and a half long. These leaves have longer petioles.

Despite the species name, the perennial root system bears tubers (a thickened branch having numerous buds or eyes) rather than a bulb (a leaf bud with fleshy scales or coats).

A cluster of white flowers on individual stalks crowd the top of the stem. Each flower may be as much as an inch across. Its four petals in the shape of long ovals form a cross, typical of the mustard family. Four greenish sepals with white edges tend to drop earlier than the petals.

The fruit is an inch-long flattened tube, pointed at each end and containing several tiny seeds.

A similar but smaller purple-flowered species, *C. douglassii*, (Torr.) Britt., usually flowers 2 weeks earlier. It is found in the northern part of our area. Some other species are also found in the state. Some of these are native; some are introductions from Europe.

Young shoots and leaves of spring cress were used by pioneers to give a biting taste to salads and as cooked greens. The base of the stem and the tubers were used as a mild horse radish substitute. Similar use by Indians is probable but not verified. Pioneers and Indians frequently exchanged information on various plants they considered valuable for food or medicinal use. Some of the species are considered a substitute for water cress.

No medical use of this species is known.

. . . photograph by Kitty Kohout

Other common names: blowballs, doonhead, lion's tooth, puffball.

Taraxacum: probably from the ancient Arabic name for the plant, *tharakhchakon.*

Officinale: from Latin meaning generally "of the shops" or "sold in the marketplace."

Daisy family: *Asteraceae (Compositae).*

Found throughout the state under a wide range of conditions, generally the full sunlight of lawns, pastures and open woods. Blooms March to frost.

Leaves form a basal rosette which may vary from nearly erect to reclining. Individual leaves may be as much as a foot long and 2 inches wide. Margins are coarsely indented with irregular teeth on the indentations. Plant parts have characteristic milky juice. The deep white taproot is perennial.

Each golden flowerhead of this persistent lawn pest tops its own slender hollow flower stalk. Stalks with heads in bud, flower and seed stages are often present at one time on a single plant. Flowerheads are usually about an inch across. Each head is a large "button" of strap-like ray flowers. Their glowing orange-yellow provides a delicate sunburst of beauty when examined closely and without prejudice.

Individual flowers each produce a tiny pin-head seed with a distinct beak. From the beak, several long soft cottony hairs protrude. A circle of greenish bracts closes while the seeds develop. As seed mature, the bracts re-open permitting the white hairs to form the familiar "puffball" ready to distribute seeds on the first strong breeze.

Dandelions have the ability to produce fertile seed without fertilization. Most of the seed in some areas is produced in this manner. (See pussytoes, *Antennaria,* for similar reproduction.) Plants produced in this manner are a genetic carbon copy of the parent. This results in loss of most ability to adapt to long term changes in environment. Perhaps at this moment, the dandelion considers itself such a success that it no longer needs to improve itself.

From ancient times, leaves of dandelion have been used for salads and cooked greens. Flowers were used to produce a wine which may have diuretic as well as alcoholic effects. The fleshy taproot served as a cooked vegetable and as a coffee substitute. Medicinally, dandelion was regarded as a treatment for jaundice, constipation, indigestion, urinary troubles, and other ailments.

When pioneers introduced the plant from Europe for some of these same purposes, American Indians soon copied their practices. The Ojibwa favored dandelion for heartburn. Kiowa women boiled the blossoms along with pennyroyal leaves to make a tea to relieve the cramps and pain of menstruation. Chippewas used a tea of roots for diseases of women.

Apaches sometimes made long journeys to procure a favorite food – dandelion leaves.   ...*photograph by Charles S. Hoffman*

Other common names: ground squirrel peas, helmet pod, rheumatism root, yellow root.

Jeffersonia: in honor of Thomas Jefferson, third president of United States and early naturalist.

Diphylla: from Latin meaning "two-leaved" in reference to the division of each leaf into two wing-like segments.

Barberry family: *Berberidaceae.*

Found throughout the state, although less frequently in the southern third, on humus-rich soils of open woodlands. It often appears in colonies along with bloodroot. Blooms April and May.

This unique perennial grows to perhaps 8 inches tall at flowering time, perhaps twice that at maturity. A slender reddish-gray petiole arising from ground level is topped by a distinctive leaf measuring as much as 6 inches long and 4 inches across at maturity. The leaves are still much smaller than that when the plant is in flower. Each leaf is divided into two similar leaflets giving a shape resembling that of a butterfly and providing a basis for the common name twinleaf. Margins of the leaf segments are generally smooth. Or they may have shallow rounded teeth which give a slightly wavy outline.

The perennial root system is a dense fibrous mat of wavy rootlets. Their light tan color gives rise to the common name yellow root used in some localities.

A delicate white flower about an inch across resembles that of bloodroot. Its stalk arises from ground level as do the leaf petioles. The eight flat petals are slender ovals. Four green sepals drop early. The flower itself is short-lived.

The unusual fruit is an upside down pear shape about an inch long. An opening toward the top extends about half way around the capsule forming a hinged "lid." It contains several rows of small brown seeds.

Both Indians and pioneers made medicinal use of twinleaf. A root tea was considered good for rheumatism, giving rise to the common name rheumatism root. Other uses included treating for syphillis, cramps, ulcers, mild cases of scarlet fever, muscle spasms, and sore throat. It was also thought to induce vomiting and to increase urine flow. Indians of the Meskwaki tribe used the root of twinleaf in a treatment for eczema and other skin problems.

The only other species of this genus is found in Asia. Our species is often included in wild flower gardens because of its unusual foliage as well as its beautiful flower.

. . . photograph by Sylvan T. Runkel

False rue anemone: *Isopyrum biternatum* (Raf.) T.&G.

Other common names: no others are known.

Isopyrum: from Greek for "like wheat" since its seeds often resemble small wheat kernels.

Biternatum: from Latin for "twice in sets of three" referring to leaves and their leaflet subdivisions.

Buttercup family: *Ranunculaceae.*

Found throughout the state in moist to medium moist woodlands, often growing in large patches. Flowers April and May.

This smooth slender perennial grows to 1½ feet tall. Its erect stem and branches have a distinct green color. The generally fibrous root system may have scattered tubers from which new plants arise. In contrast the tubers of the woodland anemone (*Anemone quinquefolia* L.) and rue anemone (*Anemonella thalictroides* L. Spach.) tend to occur in clusters. Although the roots are shallow and slender, they are tough and hardy – sometimes to the extent of maintaining green leaves all winter under the snow.

The thin leaves are mostly divided in three segments, each of which may be divided into three leaflets. So the total leaf usually has either three or nine leaflets. Each leaflet is somewhat rounded in shape, with three lobes that are deeper cut than those of the true rue anemone *(Anemonella).* The lower leaves are on long green petioles and leaf segments have stalks of their own. Uppermost leaves are often without petioles and usually with only three leaflets, each with its own short stem.

The white flowers of false rue anemone are among the earliest of spring. They tend to be earlier than, but hard to distinguish from, those of the true rue anemone and of the woodland anemone. Flowers of woodland anemone occur one per stem, while those of both false rue anemone and rue·anemone occur in loose clusters of a few flowers. The flowers, to a half inch or more across, have five white petal-like sepals, but no true petals. They are borne singly on slender flower stalks arising from axils of the uppermost leaves. Numerous (usually 10 to 40) stamens cluster in the center of the flower. Pearl-like buds give the plant an unusual beauty even before the flowers open.

The oval to oblong seed pods join to form a spreading head. Each pod contains two or three tiny smooth seeds. Individual seeds, perhaps one-eighth inch long, are tipped with a beak perhaps one half of that length.

No medicinal or food uses of this plant by Indians or pioneers are known. But both probably welcomed the false rue anemone flowers as an early sign of the abundant food supply the woodlands would provide during the following spring, summer and autumn months. 			*. . . photograph by Alvin F. Bull*

Other common names: mayflower, wild potato, wind flower.

Anemone: from a Greek term meaning "wind", probably referring to the distribution of seeds by the wind from the cottony seedheads of this genus. Or perhaps because delicate leaves and stems of some species tremble in the wind. Some authorities believe the origin goes back to a Semitic word for the mythological Adonis.

Species: Five or six of the world's more than 100 species are found in the state. Among the more common are the wood anemone (*A. quinquefolia* L.) which is pictured, Canada anemone (*A. canadensis* L.), and tall anemone (*A. virginiana* L.).

Buttercup family: *Ranunculaceae*.

Found mostly in the northern part of the state often growing in colonies in various woodland and prairie environments. Blooms April into July, depending upon the species.

The wood anemone (*A. quinquefolia* L.) is the earliest and smallest woodland anemone. The flowering stem grows about 9 inches tall with three deeply cut leaves (actually bracts) about halfway up the stem. Each leaf-like bract has its own petiole. After flowering, a basal leaf develops. The outer two of its three parts are so deeply cut it often appears five-parted to casual observation.

Each stem is topped by a solitary flower, as much as an inch across, with four to nine white to purplish sepals. It has no true petals, but the petal-like sepals give this flower a delicate beauty uniquely suited to early spring. These sepals are narrow ovals surrounding a central knob covered with numerous stamens and pistils.

Canada anemone (*A. canadensis* L.) flowers a few weeks later and grows up to 2 feet tall. It prefers a more moist soil, often appearing in thickets and the more open areas. The bracts part way up the stem are without petioles, unlike the wood anemone.

It's solitary white flower, sometimes tipped with pink or lavender is carried above the leaf-like bracts. The flower with its five sepals (again, no true petals) measures up to 1½ inches across. Individual sepals are broader than in wood anemone, making the flower appear a little more cup-like and less star-like.

A. virginiana, called thimbleweed or tall anemone, flowers still later and has fruits shaped as thimbles.

Meskwaki Indians made a tea of anemone roots for headache, dizziness – and even for refocusing of crossed eyes. It now seems likely that there was no more than psychological value in any of these uses.

One ancient legend tells that an anemone sprang up where each teardrop of the mythological Venus struck the earth as she mourned the death of her beloved Adonis.

photogragh by Sylvan T. Runkel

Dutchman's breeches: *Dicentra cucullaria* (L.) Bernh.

Other common names: boy britches, butterfly banners, colic weed, Indian boys and girls, kitten breeches, little blue staggers, white hearts.

Dicentra: from Greek meaning generally "two-spurred", for the two legs of the flower "breeches."

Cucullaria: from Latin meaing "hooded," for the tips of a pair of petals which join over the inner parts of the flower.

Poppy family: *Papaveraceae* (sometimes classed within a sub-family, *Fumarioideae.* Some botanists prefer to place this species in a separate family, *Fumariaceae.*)

Found throughout the state on rich soils of medium to moist woodlands. Blooms April and May.

Smooth slender stems arise from a common point about ground level to a height of 4 to 12 inches. Each stem, actually a leaf petiole, is topped with a smooth three-divided leaf. Each of the three parts is further deeply cut into linear segments. The resulting almost fern-like shape and their blue-green, sometimes grayish, color give Dutchman's breeches leaves a distinctive appearance.

The perennial root system includes a small divided bulb that is covered with scales.

A leafless flower stalk arches higher than the leaves and carries four to 10 flowers hanging in a one-sided cluster. Individual flowers are well described by their common name. The "breeches", usually a half to three-fourths inch long, hang upside down attached at the crotch by a delicate stem to the underside of the arching flower stalk. Actually, the legs of the breeches are spurs longer than the individual flower stalk. The white of the flowers is sometimes tinged with pink. At the "belt-line" of the breeches where the petals flare apart, expect to find a bit of yellow color.

The elongated seed capsule contains 10 to 20 tiny crested seeds.

Dutchman's breeches were used in early pioneer medicine to treat urinary problems and as a poultice for skin disease. Apparently, American Indians made little if any use of this attractive and distinctive plant.

Roots of Dutchman's breeches are poisonous. Tops also contain the same toxic alkaloids, though in lesser concentration. Sometimes cattle unintentionally pull up the plants when soil is soft and wet, getting enough bulbs to be harmful. The resulting symptoms are probably the origin of the common name "little blue staggers". Since cattle seem to find the plant distasteful, they seldom eat enough of either tops or bulbs to cause problems.

This plant is often found growing in patches with its close relataive, squirrel corn (*D. canadensis* Walp.). Both are closely related to the garden bleeding heart (*D. spectabilis* Don.).

. . . photograph by Phillip Young

Bishop's cap: *Mitella diphylla* L.

Other common names: coolwort, current leaf, fairy cup, false sanicle, fringe cap, miterwort.

Mitella: from Greek *mitra,* diminuative form meaning "little cap," probably in reference to the shape of the seed capsule or of the flower.

Diphylla: from Latin meaning "two leaves" because of the two opposite leaves, rarely three, about halfway up the lone flowering stem.

Saxifrage family: *Saxifragaceae.*

Found throughout the state in shady woods on moist organic soils. Most common on cool north-facing slopes. Blooms April to early June.

Basal leaves on petioles to 4 inches long arise from the branching perennial crown. The scaly rhizomes are twisted, pinkish, and somewhat stout. Shape of leaves may vary from nearly round to heart-shaped to lobed. Those with lobes usually have three, sometimes five, distinct lobes with the central one being longer than the others. Margins are toothed, but teeth are rounded rather than sharp. Leaves range mostly from a half to 2 inches long, slightly less in width. Leaves are hairy beneath, sparsely hairy above.

Two opposite leaves about halfway up the flowering stem are without petioles or with petioles that are quite short. Occasionaly, a third leaf occurs slightly above this pair. Stem leaves are usually smaller than basal leaves but their shape is similar.

Five to 20 delicate white flowers on stoutish individual stalks are spaced along the top 3 to 8 inches of the stem to form the flower spike. Each tiny flower, seldom more than a quarter inch across, has five lacy petals. Close exaination to necessary to appeciate their exquiste beauty. The flowers are often said to resemble snowflakes – of course, with five instead of six points. Inconspicuous sepals are whitish. Some see a resemblance of the lacy flower to a bishop's headdress or miter.

Others credit the twin-beaked seed pod with origin of the name. The two halves of the pod split open between the beaks revealing shiny jet black seeds held in a sort of basket, giving the plant a new and different beauty later in the season.

This plant was credited with medicinal uses in early history. Whatever these uses, they apparently were discounted as ineffective long ago. Any specific uses by Indians or pioneers are not known.

Bishop's cap is still chosen for some woodland flower gardens by those who take the time to apreciate its dainty beauty.

. . . photograph by LeRoy G. Pratt

Buttercup: *Ranunculus* many species

Other common names: bachelor button, blister plant, butter cresses, butter daisy, butter rose, crowfoot, horse gold, yellow yowan.

Ranunculus: from Latin for "little frog", probably because plants grow in wet areas where frogs are also found.

Species: More than a dozen of the 275 species known worldwide are found in the state. Many are so similar that technical differences between seeds are the major means of identification.

Buttercup family: *Ranunculaceae.*

Found throughout the state in wet areas, often growing in shallow water. Blooms April through September, depending upon the species.

Buttercup plants vary widely by the species. They may be annual or perennial. Stems may be reclining or erect, sometimes to 3 feet tall. New roots often start where stem nodes touch the ground. Most stems are branched. Some are smooth; some are fuzzy. Root systems are fibrous and sometimes extensive. Leaves, alternate along the stem, are divided into three parts in most species. These parts vary from thread-like to almost circular with shallow rounded teeth.

Scattered flowers grow singly at the end of a stalk which arises from among the the leaves. Frequently, a second stem arises from the same point and bears more leaves and its own stalk and flower.

Flowers generally have five yellow petals and five green sepals, but the number may vary. Early species usually are a bright yellow which glistens in the sun as if waxed or vanished. Mostly, the flowers are about an inch across. Later species tend to have smaller and less conspicuous greenish flowers with only a hint of yellow. This genus typically has numerous stamens and pistils in the center of the flower.

Some tribes of Indians pulverized buttercup roots, soaked the pulp in warm water, and used the resulting liquid as a wash for open wounds. Canadian Indians inhaled the vapor of crushed leaves of one species to cure headache. A preparation of the roots was also used to stop persistent nosebleed. One unspecified species of buttercup was used by ancients to poison arrow tips. Another was supposed to cure lunacy, if applied to the neck during the wane of the moon provided the moon was in the sign of the bull or the scorpion.

Pliny the elder, ancient Roman naturalist and writer (23-79 A.D.), is reported to have written that the buttercup "stirs him who eats it into gales of laughter. In fact, he may guffaw his way into the next world in a most unseemly manner – unless he washes the buttercup down with pineapple (?) kernels and pepper."

Some buttercups are poisonous to touch and may cause blisters. Some are poisonous to livestock, but lose their poisonous property when cut and dried for hay. Animals seldon eat buttercups when other forage is available, probably because of their bitter taste.   *...photograph by Alvin F. Bull*

Green dragon: *Arisaema dracontium* (L.) Schott.

Other common names: dragon root.

Arisaema: from the Greek words *aris*, a kind of arum, and *haema*, meaning "blood."

Dracontium: from Latin meaning "of the dragons", probably because the deeply divided leaves suggest a set of dragon claws.

Arum or calla family: *Araceae.*

Found throughout the state, mostly in cool moist shady woodland areas protected from livestock. This fragile and unique plant is now quite rare. Blooms April and May.

This unusual perennial grows to 3 feet or more tall. Each stem is topped by a single leaf subdivided into five to 15 segments arranged in a sort of semi-circle. Each segment is more or less lance-shaped, generally 3 to 10 inches long and less than an inch to 4 inches wide. The smooth almost shiny leaf segments have smooth margins. With sufficient effort, one can imagine the semi-circle of these segments to be the giant claws of a dragon foot reaching up out of the ground.

A few fibrous rootlets branch from clusters of corms. These corms provide the food storage necessary for overwintering.

Flowering parts of the green dragon branch off the main stem. The lower part is wrapped in a tube-like green spathe from which the long tail-like yellow spadix extends to 8 inches upward – sometimes to a point higher than the leaves. Some say the spadix resembles (faintly) a breath of fire exhaled by a dragon head which is represented by the spathe.

Tiny flowers on the spadix are male above, female on the lower part. Fertilized female flowers develop into shiny green fruits which ripen to a flaming red-orange in the fall. The showy fruit cluster resembles that of jack-in-the-pulpit and is a striking addition to the fall woodland scene. Each fruit contains one to three seeds.

Indians used the bulb-like corms for food. But they never ate them raw – which was to invite a fiery assault on the taste buds. The Indians learned that, by drying the corm, the unpleasant after-effects were removed (by decomposing the concentration of calcium oxalate).

Medicinally, the plant has been used interchangeably with jack-in-the-pulpit. One additional report indicates that some early folk medicine recommendations included chewing green dragon leaves to relieve symptoms of asthma.

. . . photograph by Carol J. Bull

Marsh marigold: *Caltha palustris* L.

Other common names: bitter flowers, boots, bull flower, capers, cow lily, cowslip, crazy Bet, drum hards, king's cup, meadow boots, soldier's buttons, water goggles, water boots, water gowan.

Caltha: from old Greek, and later Latin, meaning "chalice" or "cup."

Palustris: from Latin meaning "of the marsh" in reference to where the plant is usually found.

Buttercup family: *Ranunculaceae.*

Found mostly in the northern two-thirds of the state on wet soils of marshes, woodlands and stream edges. Blooms April and May.

A soft, spongy perennial root system with masses of fine rootlets gives rise to bunches of stout juicy stems, mostly growing erect to 2 feet tall.

The stems are hollow and furrowed giving a somewhat angular appearance. Upper parts of the stem are usually branched. The smooth glossy lower leaves have long petioles. They are kidney-shaped to broadly heart-shaped, measuring as much as 8 inches across. Upper leaves are smaller, often with short petioles. The leaves are smooth and dark green with wavy margins but no teeth. Veins are conspicuous.

Bright yellow flowers, to 1½ inch across, may put on a spectacular display in April and May. The flower has no petals, but five to nine colorful sepals appear as petals. Each sepal is broadly oval in shape. Together they form a shallow cup surrounding numerous stamens. This cup shape provides the basis for the name of the genus.

In early medicine, the plant was used to treat dropsy, anemia, convulsions, and coughing. A drop of juice was squeezed daily on a wart to cause its disappearance. Indians used the plant to treat colds, diseases of women, and scrofulous sores.

Leaves (gathered in the spring, before the flowers bloom, and thoroughly cooked to destroy a toxic alkaloid) were widely used as greens by northern Indians and pioneers. Livestock have been poisoned by eating excessively of the plants when other forage was unavailable.

Flower buds were pickled and were considered a delicacy. Blossoms have been used to make wine. They were also a source of yellow dye.

In Irish folklore, the *Caltha* took on extra significance on May Day when witches and fairies were supposed to be particularly active. Bunches of *Caltha*, known locally as mayflower, were hung over doorways to protect fertility of cattle.

The marigold term probably comes from an old Anglo Saxon term meaning "horse blister". The common name in parts of England is "horse blob", blob being dialect for blister.

The term cowslip is probably from "cow slop" indicating that the plant grows better where cows have dropped their dung.

. . . photograph by Sylvan T. Runkel

Squirrel corn: *Dicentra canadensis* Walp.

Other common names: colic weed, turkey pea, wild hyacinth.

Dicentra: from Greek meaning "two spurred", referring to the two flower spurs which are prominent in some species.

Canadensis: meaning "of Canada."

Poppy family: *Papaveraceae (sometimes classed within a sub-family, Fumarioideae.* Some botanists prefer to place this species in a separate family, *Fumariaceae.)*

Found on rich moist soils of open woodlands throughout the state. Often found growing with its close relative, Dutchman's breeches – *D. cucullaria* (L.) Bernh. Blooms April and May.

Slender smooth stems (actually leaf petioles) grow from a common point about ground level to as tall as one foot. Each is topped with a three-parted leaf. Each division is deeply cut into numerous linear segments, giving a fern-like appearance that is quite distinctive. The leaves closely resemble those of Dutchman's breeches except for being finer, more delicate, more compact, and more grayish in color.

The perennial root system resembles a necklace of small orange-yellow tubers. The tubers are pea-sized, often described as looking like kernels of corn. Small white rootlets grow from each tuber. The common name may have come from this resemblance and from the fact that the plants grow where squirrels are common.

The small white flowers are more heart-shaped and lack the spreading spurs of Dutchman's breeches. This species has shorter, more rounded spurs that are much less conspicuous. They much more closely resemble a white version of the common garden "bleeding heart" *D. spectabilis* (L.) D.C. The yellowish crest of the inner petals is projecting and prominent. Four to eight flowers droop on short slender stalks as elongated heart-shaped pendants below the main flower stalk which arches gracefully above the leaves. Individual flowers are commonly about three-fourths of an inch long and less than one half inch across.

Squirrel corn flowers have a slight but pleasing hyacinth fragrance. Their generally white color may be either somewhat greenish or tinged with pink.

The elongated two-valved seed capsule contains many tiny crested seeds.

This plant is poisonous, but to a lesser degree than Dutchman's breeches. It is likely that both species contain the same toxic alkaloids. Mice particularly like to eat the tubers and seem to be unaffected by the toxicity.

No food or medicinal uses of this species by Indians and pioneers are known. But in early European medicine, it was used to treat skin problems, syphilis, scrofula, and some menstrual complaints.

. . . photograph by LeRoy G. Pratt

Bellwort: *Uvularia grandiflora* J. E. Smith.

Other common names: merrybells, Mohawk weed, straw-bells, wild oats, yellow bellwort.

Uvularia: from Latin for the small conical body in the center of the human palate, referring to the flower which hangs from its stalk like the human uvula from the palate.

Grandiflora: from Latin meaning "big flower."

Lily family: *Liliaceae.*

Found throughout the state on rich soils of heavily shaded uplands and slopes. It often grows in colonies but seldom in pure stands. Blooms April into June.

The smooth stem grows erect to 20 inches tall. It is usually forked, but only one branch carries flowers as well as leaves. After flowering, the stem elongates in a somewhat zigzag fashion, slightly changing angle at each leaf joint. Oblong to oval leaves as much as 5 inches long occur alternately along the stem. Usually only one or two leaves are found below the fork. The sterile branch usually has four to eight leaves.

Leaves have smooth margins and parallel veins. The leaves have no petioles and their bases tend to loop around the stem. The leaves are scarcely unfolded at flowering. This gives the plant a twisted droopy wilted appearance. The leaves may be whitish and slightly hairy beneath.

The perennial rootstock is a short horizontal rhizome with fleshy rootlets.

Lemon yellow flowers droop like long twisted bells on individual flower stalks along the end of the stem. Only rarely do two flowers occur together. Three yellow sepals join three yellow petals to form blossoms one to 2 inches long. The sepals and petals are somewhat pointed and curved to one side giving the entire flower a unique twisted appearance.

The fruit is a small three-angled capsule usually less than a half inch long.

Early settlers cooked the upper stems and leaves as greens. Young shoots served as a substitute for asparagus. The roots, too, have been cooked as food.

In early medicine, this plant was used to produce a general stomach remedy and as a poultice for wounds and skin inflammations. Canker sores in the mouth were treated with a concoction made from the roots.

Whether or not Indians made similar food and medical uses of yellow bellwort is not known. It is likely they learned of both from the pioneers if they lacked prior knowledge of their own. Exchange of such knowledge was frequent.

In early European medicine, this plant was considered a treatment for throat problems relating to the palate or uvula, following the ancient "doctrine of signatures."

Another species, *U. sessilifolia* L., with slightly smaller flowers and leaves which do not clasp the stem is found mostly in the southern part of the state.   *. . . photograph by Marvin Dove*

Wild ginger: *Asarum canadense* L.

Other common names: asarabacca, catfoot, colic root, false colt's foot, ginger root, heart snakeroot, Indian ginger.

Asarum: from Greek, the ancient name of a European species.

Canadense: meaning "of Canada."

Birthwort family: *Aristolochiaceae.*

Found throughout the state, usually in extensive colonies, in cool shady woodlands where soils are moist in the springtime. Flowers April and May.

Large leaves, usually two, grow on hairy petioles frequently 6 inches or more long. They may be erect or reclining. The petioles arise directly from an unusual perennial rootstock. It is horizontal, partly buried, and much branched. It shows prominent scars of previous leaf growth. A spicy ginger-like aroma is obvious when the root is crushed. This, of course, provides the basis for some of the common names applied to this species.

Each dark green leaf, as much as 7 inches across, is deeply indented at the petiole to form a crude heart or kidney shape. Margins are smooth and veining is prominent.

In the notch of the two leaf petioles, a single flower droops on its own hairy stalk so close to the ground that it is sometimes buried in the forest duff. The bell-shaped flower is an unusual maroon to rich brown color inside, somewhat lighter outside. It is dull, rather than shiny, and covered with stiff white hairs.

The flower has no petals, but three pointed sepals join toward their bases to form the cup. These sepals are rather thick—more fleshy than one usually expects of petals or sepals. The cup may be as much as an inch across, usually less.

The fruit is a fleshy, six-celled capsule which bursts to free numerous tiny seeds. The capsule is generally less than three-fourths of an inch across.

Pioneers have used the roots and rhizomes as substitutes for Jamaica ginger which was hard to acquire. True ginger of the spice shelf is derived from a different plant, *Zingiber officinale,* which grows only in the tropics. The rhizomes were sometimes boiled with sugar to make a natural candied spice. In early medicine, wild ginger was highly regarded as a treatment for whooping cough. It has also been used for digestive stomach upset, chest complaints, fevers, heart palpitations, and many other ailments.

Indian women of one tribe are said to have considered wild ginger tea to be a contraceptive. Chippewas used it in food to treat indigestion. Chopped up on a plantain leaf, it served as a poultice for inflammations of the skin. (An active antibiotic substance has been isolated from the plant so this treatment had a sound medical basis.)

For the Meskwaki, wild ginger was probably the most important native seasoning. They also thought its use eliminated danger of poisoning when eating an animal that had died of unknown causes. They also chewed the root and spit it upon bait to improve the chances of catching fish.

. . . photograph by Leroy G. Pratt

Dogtooth violet: *Erythronium albidum* Nutt

Other common names: adder's tongue, deer tongue, lamb tongue, thousand leaf, white fawn lily, white trout lily.

Erythronium: from Greek for "red" because the genus name comes from a red-flowered species found in Europe.

Albidum: from Latin for "white." Yellow-flowered species, *E. americanum, Ker.* is also found throughout Indiana and areas to the east.

Lily family: *Liliaceae.*

Found throughout the state in rich mosit woodlands, especially in bottomlands with open woods. Colonies of plants may be extensive. Blooms April to June.

Paired leaves, as much as 8 inches long and 1½ inches wide, arise from a mostly underground stem. They are broadly lance-shaped, thick and smooth – almost shiny. Young leaves are often mottled with brown on the upper surface, lighter in color beneath. The leaves, without marginal teeth, curve in a graceful arc. They show a distinct mid-rib, almost as if they had been folded lengthwise.

For the first 2 or 3 years, only a tiny single leaf is produced. The next 2 or 3 years, a larger leaf is produced. Thereafter, two leaves are formed. But a new plant may not flower until 6 or 7 years old – always after it starts producing two leaves.

The perennial root system is a deeply buried bulb which sends out long shoots to produce new plants. So it is usually found in patches of a few to hundreds of plants. Colonies of leaves appear 2 to 4 weeks before the flowers, giving rise to the common name "thousand leaf."

A nodding star of a flower is carried on a single leafless stalk which arises from between the paired leaves. Three petals and three sepals look so much alike the flower appears to have six petals. They open from a straight tight bud to a strongly re-curved star-like appearance. Individual petals or sepals may be as much as 2 inches long. Prominent veins are parallel to the tip. Flowers, averaging perhaps an inch across, are white with a tinge of pink, rarely with strong shades of blue or purple.

The bulbs, up to 1½ inch in diameter, provided food for many tribes of Indians who ate them raw, boiled, or roasted. Their flavor is crisp, clean, and somewhat sweet. While pioneers knew of the edible bulbs, they found that the effort required for digging the small bulbs limited their value as a source of food. The yellow species, and probably the white species, was considered a treatment for gout.

Small burrowing animals of the woodlands also depend upon the bulbs for food.

If the flower and two leaves are picked, the plant dies. In its short growing season it cannot produce new leaves to replenish the food reserves in the bulb. Such food storage is necessary for the plant to overwinter and send up new growth the following spring. *...photograph by Nancy Dove*

Blue cohosh: *Caulophyllum thalictroides (L.)* Michx.

Other common names: blueberry root, blue ginseng, papoose root, squaw root.

Caulophyllum: from Greek *kaulos* meaning "stem" and from *phyllum* meaning "leaf".

Thalictroides: from close resemblance of leaves to those of meadow rue, *Thalictrum.*

Barberry family: *Berberidaceae.*

Found throughout the state in rich shady woodlands where moisture is plentiful – usually in well-drained bottomlands. Blooms in April and May.

This smooth slender perennial grows to 3 feet tall. The distinctive blue-green to purplish color of the early growth helps to identify it. The plant usually has but a single leaf toward the top of the stem. This single large leaf is divided into three parts, each of which is subdivided into three segments. The result appears more like nine separate leaflets. Each of these leaflets has three lobes.

This compound leaf is almost without a true petiole, providing the basis for the generic name. The entire leaf may be 2 feet or more across. In some instances, a second smaller leaf may appear at the base of the flowerhead. This leaf has two subdivisions, each with three leaflets.

The perennial rootstock is matted, knotty, and rather thick. Since only a single stem is produced during a season, one could determine the age of the plant by counting the scars which previous growth has left on the upper side of the rootstock.

The tiny flowers, less than a half inch across, are borne in terminal clusters on a flower stalk rising slightly above the leaf. The flowers appear early, before the leaf reaches its full size. The six petals are green to yellowish-green, sometimes tinged with red. The petals are thick and gland-like, smaller than and opposite to the green sepals. The colorful fruits on short stems each contain two seeds and resemble blueberries when ripe. They are not true berries – rather seeds which have developed a protective fleshy covering.

Both Indian and pioneer medicine found many uses for blue cohosh. The Omaha tribe made a tea for treating fever. The Meskwaki named the root "a woman" and from it brewed a tea for treating genito-urinary disorders. Many tribes used this plant to facilitate childbirth. A root tea taken during the week or two prior to childbirth was supposed to give rapid and comparatively painless delivery.

Pioneers tried blue cohosh treatments for rheumatism, epilepsy, colic, and many other disabilities. At one time, roots and rhizomes were actively collected for use by early pharmacists in preparing medicines.

The berries, if eaten, are irritating to mucous membranes – and may cause other troubles. One report, however, indicates that the berries can be roasted and used as a sort of coffee substitute. Some people develop a rash from contact with the plant.

. . . photograph by Sylvan T. Runkel

Goldenseal: *Hydrastis canadensis* L.

Other common names: eye balm, eye root, ground raspberry, Indian dye, orange root, tumeric root, yellow eye, yellow Indian paint, yellow puccoon, yellow root.

Hydrastis: from Greek *hydro* meaning "water", probably originating from *Hydrophyllum canadense* with which this plant was once confused.

Canadensis: meaning "of Canada."

Buttercup family: *Ranunculaceae.*

Found infrequently throughout the state, growing in small patches on rich well drained soils where natural woods provide open shade. Flowers April and May.

In early spring, a thick hairy stem grows 6 to 20 inches tall from a thick perennial yellow rootstock. A single basal leaf on a long petiole grows perhaps 8 inches wide. Two smaller stem leaves (actually bracts) are borne alternately without petioles near the top of the main stem. The upper stem leaf is just below the flower. Each leaf has five to nine deeply cut lobes with coarse teeth. After flowering, additional leaves on long petioles arise directly from the roots. The leaves somewhat resemble those of the raspberry, part of the basis for one of the common names. Their deep green color and coarsely textured surface provide a distinctive appearance.

The perennial rhizome is a thick oblong shape, knotty and irregular. It has a thin yellow-brown bark and a bright yellow interior. Numerous rootlets branch from the rhizome.

A single inconspicuous greenish-white flower about a half inch across rises above the top leaf on a short stalk. The unusual flower has no petals and only three sepals which drop off as the flower opens. Numerous stamens (male flower parts) and pistils (female parts) form a dense head. The flower is followed by a fruit resembling the red raspberry. It contains 10 to 20 small hard shiny black seeds.

Both Indians and pioneers used goldenseal as a tonic, stimulant, and astringent. It also served as a treatment for sore throat, sore eyes, and mouth ulcers. The liquid from goldenseal root boiled in water was used as a wash for skin diseases.

Cherokee Indians pounded the rootstock into bearfat and used the resulting salve as an insect repellant. The Meskwaki and Potawatomi tribes used it to make a treatment for eczema and an inhalant for catarrh. A yellow dye derived from the root was used to color clothes and weapons.

Pioneers used goldenseal as a home remedy for stomach ailments and as a laxative. They and their early doctors often carried seeds with them when they moved to new areas.

The goldenseal plant is considered poisonous, causing ulcer and inflammation of mucous membranes if taken internally. The plant is cultivated commercially as a source of medicines. Herb gatherers have made the plant increasingly rare in our woodlands.   *...photograph by Marlin Bowles*

Other common names: American sanicle, cliffweed, ground maple, rock geranium.

Heuchera: in honor of Johann Heinrich von Heucher, an early German physician and botanist who wrote extensively on medical botany.

Richardsonii: In honor of Sir John Richardson who explored North America in the 19th century. Species of *Heuchera* may hybridize and make identification rather difficult.

Saxifrage family: *Saxifragaceae.*

Found throughout the state, mostly on the drier soils of rocky wooded areas and on the sandy soils in prairie type environments. Flowers April to June.

Attractive basal leaves, shaped somewhat like those of the hard maple tree, are carried on long petioles (leaf stems) which arise from a perennial crown. Each leaf, 2 to 3 inches across, has five to nine rounded shallow lobes with coarsely toothed margins. Tiny bristly white hairs line the veins on the underside of the leaves. Leaf petioles are covered with shaggy white hairs. In those cases where leaves appear along the flower stalk, they are widely spaced and alternate.

Fibrous rootlets branch from a coarse black perennial rootstock.

Flowering stalks, usually leafless and covered with shaggy white hairs, grow mostly one to 2 feet tall and stand well above the leaves. Somewhat bell-shaped flowers, perhaps a quarter inch long, droop on individual short stalks branching from the main flower stalk. Five spatula-shaped petals of white to pale green, sometimes lavender, may be irregular at their outer ends. The upper petals tend to be slightly longer than the lower ones. Stamens (male flower parts) tipped with brilliant orange anthers extend outward beyond the "bell" of the flower. Five green sepals, nearly as large as the petals, are often quite unequal in size. The flowering spike may occupy as much as the top third of its stalk.

The fruit is a small dry oval capsule forming a single cell which contains several tiny seeds.

Both Indians and pioneers pounded dried roots of this species into a powder and applied it as an astringent to close wounds that were difficult to heal. The powder was also used to treat diarrhea and sore throat. The Meskwaki tribe also gathered the green leaves to make an astringent dressing for open sores.

The common name alumroot comes from the puckering alum-like taste of the root. The wild geranium is also called alumroot in some localities because of its similar astringent properties.

Perhaps best known of this genus is the cultivated garden plant called coral bells, *H. sanguinea* Engelm. The appearance is similar except that the flowers of coral bells generally vary from pink or rose to deep crimson.

H. americana L. is common throughout Indiana. *H. parviflora* Bartl. and *H. villosa* Michx. are found only in southern counties.   *...photograph by W.K. Hollingsworth*

Blue-eyed Mary: *Collinsia verna* Nutt.

Other common names: broadleaf collinsia, innocence.

Collinsia: in honor of Zaccheus Collins, early American botanist and vice president of the Philadelphia Academy of Science.

Verna: from Latin meaning "of spring", referring to the time of flowering. Other species of this native American genus are found mostly in western states.

Snapdragon family: *Scrophulariaceae.*

Found sparingly, throughout the state, on rich moist soils of woodlands and thickets – especially along streams. Flowers April to June.

This thin delicate annual wilts easily. It grows 6 to 24 inches tall, mostly unbranched except from the base. Widely spaced leaves, usually one to 2 inches long, grow opposite along the weak stem. Upper leaves are somewhat lance-shaped and may tend to wrap around the stem. Lower leaves are broader – more egg-shaped – and on long petioles. Leaf margins may be either smooth or toothed. The foliage dies early – usually in July – not long after flowering.

Colorful blue and white flowers cluster in loose whorls of about six blossoms around the top of the stem. Other flower stalks emerge from axils of upper leaves. Individual snapdragon-like flowers about a half inch long have two white upper lobes and three lower lobes of rich blue or violet.

The middle lobe of the lower lip is folded lengthwise and almost disappears between the outer two. The resulting pouch encloses the reproductive parts, a style and four stamens. Individual flower stalks are longer than the flower themselves.

The small oval seed capsule has two compartments each containing one or two thick but tiny wrinkled seeds. Small patches of plants come up from seeds dropped the previous year. The seeds may start growing in the fall and complete their development the following spring.

Despite the fact that this species produces few seeds, it reproduces freely under favorable garden conditions. This indicates that the seeds must have both high germination and unusual vigor.

No food or medicinal uses of this species by Indians or pioneers are known. It is frequently selected for flower gardens because of its distinctive beauty and unusual coloring. It is surprising that so little has been written about this plant in view of these characteristics.   *...photograph by John Schwegman*

Other common names: Indian turnip.

Arisaema: from two Greek woods *aris*, a kind of arum and from *haema* meaning "blood."

Triphyllum: from Latin meaning "three leaves."

Arum or calla family: *Araceae.*

Found throughout the state, mostly in low moist woods but sometimes on pockets of rich soil on steep slopes. This species is becoming increasingly rare. Flowers April to June.

Distinctive foliage of this plant includes one or two leaves, each with three pointed oval leaflets. These leaflets, up to 7 inches long, have smooth margins. Long petioles of the leaves arise from a deeply buried bulb-like stem base. Fibrous roots grow from the bottom of this turnip-shaped corm. This perennial corm is the plant's storehouse which provides for it's early growth the following spring. The leaf petioles generally clasp the stalk of the spathe and spadix.

A separate stalk carries the club-like spadix (commonly called the preacher or the jack). It is usually 2 or 3 inches long and covered by minute yellow flowers. Male flowers are grouped above the female flowers. (Some botanists disagree, believing that the flowers undergo a sex change when the plant is about 3 years old. They consider the flowers first staminate, or male, changing to pistillate, or female.) A leaf-like spathe wraps around the lower part of the spadix but opens to expose the upper part. The open portion extends above the spadix and curves over it to form the "pulpit". This spathe may be green, purplish-brown, or striped.

The fruit is a showy cluster of scarlet berries, each about a quarter inch in diameter and containing four to six seeds. The colorful seed head, one to 3 inches long, is easily spotted in early autumn.

This unusual plant found many uses in Indian medicine. The Chippewas used it to treat sore eyes. Pawnees powdered the root and applied it to the head or temples for headache. It was also used to treat snakebite, ringworm, stomach gas, rheumatism, asthma, and other disorders.

The corm was also used for food. It was boiled or baked, peeled, powered, and heated again. This was necessary to inactivate the high concentration of calcium oxalate and make a mild edible flour. Others pounded the roots to a pulp with water and allowed the mass to dry for several weeks for the same purpose.

The Meskwaki also used the root in disputes with other tribes. They'd cook meat with the fresh root and abandon it hoping the opposing warriors would find it and partake of the meal – later to become sick, or even die, of calcium oxalate poisoning.

Years ago most country boys learned the hard way (encouraged by the more experienced) that tasting the raw bulb produces a severe stinging sensation described "as a mouthful of red hot needles". Apparently the concentration of calcium oxalate is the cause.   *...photograph by Eugene Held*

White baneberry: *Actaea pachypoda* Ell.

Other common names: doll's eyes, necklace weed, snakeroot, toadroot, white cohosh, white heads.

Actaea: from Greek *aktea* or *aktaia*, an ancient name for the elder tree which was transferred to this genus.

Pachypoda: from Latin meaning "thick footed" referring to the thick stems carrying flowers and fruits.

Buttercup family: *Ranunculaceae.*

Found throughout the state on rich moist soils in the moderate to deep shade of woodlands. Blooms April to June.

This leafy plant is bushy in appearance. It grows to about 2 feet tall, sometimes several stems in a clump. The large leaves are divided into three leaflets which vary in shape. Leaflets, especially the end one, may have three irregular lobes. All have sharp and irregular teeth in the margins. Leaf segments are often more than an inch across. The lower leaves have petioles while upper leaves may not. Red baneberry, *A. rubra* (Ait.) Willd., has leaves which are less pointed in appearance, darker in color, and usually fewer in number.

The extensive perennial rootstock is coarse and fibrous. It is highly poisonous.

The baneberry is inconspicuous until the single creamy white plume of flowers appears. Flowers are scattered along the flower stem in a cylindrical cluster perhaps 4 inches long. Individual flowers are tiny – each on its own stout stalk branching from the main flower stem. The stalk is usually red, but this is not always the case. Close examination of the flower shows four to 10 slender spatula-shaped petals which tend to be squared off at the tip. Flowers of red baneberry are similar, but they are on more slender stalks.

Ivory white berries form an open cluster, to 7 inches long. Each berry, to as much as a half inch across, has an unusual purple spot at the end. This, of course accounts for the common name, doll's eyes. Each berry is carried on its own stout red stem. The stoutness of this fruit stem is one key to distinguishing between an uncommon red variation of this species and the common red baneberry. In rare cases, berries of the red species may be white. Each berry usually contains five to 10 seeds. The berries are poisonous.

One descriptive Indian name translates generally as "a little sweet root . . . one nearly dies . . . is given to eat."

Cheyenne women drank a tea of baneberry leaves to increase milk secretion. As with other tribes, they often nursed a child until it was 3 or 4 years old. Chippewa Indians used white baneberry for non-specific diseases of women, and red baneberry for diseases of men.

Indians of the Northwest used a weak tea of white baneberry to wash babies. A stronger tea was brewed for treating sores.

Both Indians and pioneers made a tea of the root for relieving pain of childbirth. Pioneers also used the plant to improve circulation and to cure headache or eyestrain.

. . . photograph by LeRoy Pratt

Jacob's ladder: *Polemonium reptans* L.

Other common names: bluebell, Greek valerian, skunk weed.

Polemonium: from Greek, probably honoring the ancient philosopher Polemon. Or perhaps from the ancient Greek name for war, *polemos*. Pliny the Elder, ancient writer and naturalist, wrote that a short war occurred in an argument over who discovered this flower.

Reptans: from Latin for "creeping", not a true description of this species.

Phlox family: *Polemoniaceae*.

Found throughout the state on rich soils of moist woods and bottomlands. Blooms April to June.

Slender and rather weak low-branching stems of this plant are more or less upright, not creeping. Height is seldom much more than one foot. Loose tufts of many stems are more common than solitary stems.

Basal leaves, often without petioles, have pairs of smooth-margined locust-like leaflets which form a "ladder" along the central vein. As many as 17 pointed oval leaflets are paired opposite except for one at the tip. The total leaf may be as long as 12 inches while individual leaflets are seldom more than 1½ inches long.

Leaves along the stem are alternate and on short petioles. They have fewer and smaller leaflets than the basal leaves.

The perennial root system is a tight fibrous clump which may reach deep into the soil.

Deep blue bell-shaped flowers may be as large as one half inch across and three-fourths inch long. Flowers nod on individual stalks from long slender branches ascending above the leaves. The individual stalks are about as long as the flower. Each branch has but a few flowers in its cluster.

The flare of the flower bell has five rounded lobes. Five prominent but unequal white stamens (male flower parts), contrast with the deep blue of the "bell" to remind one of the blue and white of the Greek flag.

The fruit is a small dry capsule containing few, usually three, hard seeds.

In early medicine, this plant was often included in May apple tea to make a more effective purge for diarrhea.

Indian names for the plant often translate as something close to "smells like pine." The Menomini tribe used it to treat eczema and skin sores. The Meskwaki and Potawatami tribes made it into a treatment for hemorrhoids.

No food uses are known.

A close relative, *P. caeruleum* L., was introduced from Europe and found wide use in flower gardens. It adapted readily and is sometimes found in our woodlands as an escape from early gardens. This is a larger species, growing to 3 feet tall, and has more flowers in each cluster.

. . . photograph by W. K. Hollingsworth

One-flowered cancer root: *Orobanche uniflora* L.

Other common names: naked broomrape, one-flowered broomrape, pale broomrape, pipes, square drops.

Orobanche: From Greek meaning "strangle vetch" in reference to its parasitic habit.

Uniflora: from Latin for "one flower", in obvious reference to the fact that the plant producers but a single flower.

Broomrape family: *Orobanchaceae.*

Found, now rarely, throughout the state in damp woodlands. Blooms April to June.

A pale hairy flower stem, almost colorless, grows to 10 inches tall. Usual height is considerably less, however. It develops a parasitic attachment to the roots of other woodland plants. This does not seem to harm host plants.

As a parasite, the plant has no need for leaves or chlorophyl. (Chlorophyl is green coloring matter which uses the energy of sunlight to convert carbon dioxide, nutrients from the soil, and water into plant material.) Scale-like protrusions near the base of the stem are vestigial leaves which no longer play a part in survival of the species.

Some specialists believe that the tiny seeds are unable to germinate unless they start right against the roots of the host plant.

The actual stem is usually less than an inch long and nearly buried in the soil. One to four flower stalks arise from this horizontal stem. Many stems usually occur together forming a dense mat several inches across. As a result, many flower stalks are sometimes found clustered together.

A single fragile flower, commonly three-fourths inch long, nods atop its hairy stalk. Rarely, multiple flowers will occur on one stem. The tube-shaped flower ends in five lobes that flare outward. Usually, the tube is somewhat curved. The two lobes of the upper lip are slightly shorter than the three of the lower lip. Color varies from pale purple to light pink. Two yellow bands add a bit of color to the inside of the lower lip. The flower has a delicate violet-like fragrance. Close examination will show a sparse coating of very short hairs on the outside of the flower.

The base of the flower tube fits into a bell-shaped calyx with five sharply pointed lobed. This calyx is usually less than a half inch long.

An Asian species with many yellow and blue flowers occurs rarely as an escape from domestic plantings.

The fruit is a one-celled oval capsule that is a half to three-fourths inch long. The dried and withered flower tube often stays attached to the fruit capsule. Numerous tiny wrinkled seeds are contained in the capsule.

No medicinal or food uses of this plant by Indians or pioneers are known.   *. . . photograph by Randall A. Maas*

Showy orchis: *Orchis spectabilis* Pursh.

Other common names: gay orchis, purple orchis, spring orchis.

Orchis: from Greek word for "testicle" since some species were said to have roots resembling testicles.

Spectabilis: from Latin meaning "showy."

Orchid family: *Orchidaceae.*

Found throughout the state but becoming rare. Favors rich, damp, slightly acid to alkaline soils of undisturbed woods where shade, moisture, and other environmental factors are favorable. Flowers April to June.

The smooth and slightly five-angled stem of this spectacular plant seldom grows more than one foot tall. The erect stems are fleshy but tender and are easily broken. Plants usually occur in small dense clumps.

Two large egg-shaped leaves narrow toward their bases and clasp the stem close to ground level. Plants with one leaf or three leaves are found infrequently. Leaves vary from somewhat ascending to resting on the gound. They may be as much as 8 inches long and half as wide. They have numerous parallel veins and smooth margins.

The leaves are a lustrous clear green color; thick, smooth, and clammy to the touch. The perennial root system is fleshy and fibrous, generally somewhat coarse. The roots may lie dormant for several years and then unexpectedly produce dense clumps of plants.

Three to six orchid flowers form a spike at the top of the simple stem. Typical of orchids, these inch-long flowers have one of their three petals in peculiar form, (a fringed banner, a cornucopia containing the nectar, or a broad landing platform for insects). In the case of showy orchis, the specialized petal is a lip of the landing platform type. It is generally white, sometimes spotted, with a blunt spur at its base. This lip angles sharply downward rather than toward the horizontal as the "landing pad" term could imply.

The two lateral petals and the sepals form an arching hood over the lip. The purple to violet or rose color of the hood makes this plant one of the woodland's more beautiful inhabitants. The hood is about the same length as the spur, seldom over three-fourths of an inch. The flower has a delicate fragrance.

No medical or food uses of showy orchis by Indians and pioneers are known.

A similar species, *O. rotundifolia* Banks, is even more rare. It has a single smaller roundish leaf and lateral sepals which are distinctly spreading rather than forming part of the hood. Showy orchis is unfortunately a favorite of amateur plant collectors. It is so sensitive to changes in habitat that transplanting usually fails. Because of this, these species are becoming increasingly rare.   *...photograph by Dr. W. R. Kern*

Shooting star: *Dodecatheon meadia* L.

Other common names: American cowslip, birdbills, Johnny jump, Indian chief, pride-of-Ohio, rooster heads.

Dodecatheon: from Greek for "twelve gods", a name originally applied to another plant and later transferred to this genus.

Meadia: in honor of Dr. Richard Mead, early English physician and botanist.

Primrose family: *Primulaceae.*

Found throughout the state on rocky slopes and cliff edges of open woods. It generally prefers meadows and native prairie. Flowers April to June.

A basal rosette of leaves appears in early spring from a short fibrous perennial rootstock. The leaves, shaped somewhat like a long spatula, may be as long as 8 inches. The base and mid-rib tend to have a somewhat reddish color. The leaves narrow toward their bases, some to the extent of providing a margined or winged petiole. Leaf margins tend to be wavy, rarely with shallow coarse rounded teeth. Some of the variation may be due to differences in species or hybridizing between species.

A smooth hollow leafless flower stalk towers 6 to 20 inches above the basal leaf rosette. Toward its top it divides into several slender arching branches with individual flowers. These clusters usually contain fewer than a dozen nodding star-like flowers, but may far exceed this number.

Five narrow petals, varying from crimson to lilac to pale pink and sometimes to white, are joined at their base to form a short tube. These petals sweep outward and upward, providing the star-like shape. Stamens protrude in a beak-like cone from the center of the flower, adding a sense of speeding motion. The center of the flower is yellow with a dark circle where the yellow of the center joins the pink of the petals. Individual "stars" may be as much as three-fourths inch across.

In the fruit stage, the small dark reddish-brown barrel-shaped seed capsules are carried erect rather than drooping. The outer edge of the "barrel" has toothed edges. These seed capsules are small, usually less than a half inch long.

Few uses of this plant by Indians and pioneers are known. But its striking beauty assures that it did not go unnoticed. Some reports indicate use by Indians as an emergency food.

There is considerable disagreement among authorities about classification of plants in this genus. Some list 30 or more species over the wide area of distribution while others may list only one or two. If species are truly so few, it represents an unusually wide adaptation for single species.

. . . photograph by Marlin Bowles

Other common names: dog toes, everlasting, four toes, Indian tobacco, ladies' tobacco, pearly mouse ear, poverty weed, white plantain.

Antennaria: from Latin for "insect antenna" in reference to the appearance of projecting parts of the flowerhead of some species.

Plantaginifolia: from Latin for "plantain leaf" referring to the shape of leaves. A similar but smaller species, *A. neglecta* Greene (from Latin for "overlooked") is also found in the state.

Daisy family: *Asteraceae (Compositae).*

Found throughout the state, mostly on dry soils of open woods, pastures or meadows. Blooms April to June.

This perennial has two kinds of leaves. Basal leaves around a crown are paddle-shaped and measure to 3 inches long, 1½ inches wide. They are a dull dark green above, silver green beneath. Each leaf has three, sometimes more, prominent veins. This set of leaves has distinct petioles. Leaves along the erect stem are narrow, not more than one-fourth inch wide, and pointed. They are widely spaced and progressively smaller on the upper stem. They narrow toward their base but have no petioles. *A. neglecta* Greene is similar but smaller. Its leaves are narrower and have but a single vein.

A cluster of small dense heads of minute white tubular flowers gives a powerpuff effect to the top of the flower stalk. Individual heads are ball-shaped flower groups measuring about one quarter inch across. The stem may be as much as 20 inches tall.

Male and female flowers are on separate plants – often in patches of a single sex since the plant spreads mostly by underground stolons. Female flower heads often have a pinkish color. The white male flower heads are usually on somewhat smaller plants.

Some *Antennaria* species have developed the ability to set seed without pollen. In fact, some species have no male flowers at all. This sexless reproductive process in plants is called "apomixis."

Early folk medicine sometimes prescribed a tea of pussytoes leaves taken every day for 2 weeks after childbirth to keep the mother from getting sick. It was also thought to control hemorrhage after childbirth.

A concoction from the plant was once used to treat stomach disorders. Flowers of pussytoes have been used to make a cough syrup.

There is no record of this plant actually having been used as a tobacco substitute as some of the common names imply.

This plant often grows on poor dry soils where few others will. In such locations it serves an important function of reducing erosion by holding soil in place with its extensive root system.

. . . photograph by Sylvan T. Runkel

Sweet William: *Phlox divaricata* L.

Other common names: blue phlox.

Phlox: from Greek meaning "flame", probably from the bright colors of the flowers. This name was used in ancient times for *Lychnis* but was later transferred to this genus.

Divaricata: from Latin meaning "divergent" or "spreading" referring to the branching of the flowering head.

Phlox family: *Polemoniaceae.*

Found throughout the state in partial shade of rich moist woodlands, often in patches or colonies along streams. Flowers April to June.

Slender stems grow to 30 inches tall, mostly erect and unbranched to the flower head. Some stems may be somewhat reclining. Dark leafy shoots spread from the base and often take root at the nodes. Leaves on these shoots are leathery and may retain some brownish-green color throughout the year. The upper stems tend to be somewhat hairy and sticky. This serves the phlox plant in much the same way a man-made caterpillar barrier serves a tree.

Leaves along the hairy stems occur opposite in widely spaced pairs. They are oval or lance-shaped, to 2 inches long,and with little or no petiole. The perennial root system is tough, fibrous, and stringy.

A loose cluster of showy blue to violet, sometimes white, flowers occur at the top of the stem. Individual flowers are slender tubes with five petal-like lobes. Lobes may be either rounded or with a shallow notch. Shape and depth of the notch may show considerable variation. Each lobe narrows toward the tube giving a distinct wedge shape. Individual flowers may be three-fourths of an inch or more across. Flowers are noted for their color, beauty, and fragrance.

The fruit is a small oval capsule with two or three compartments and a single seed per compartment.

Many other species of phlox may be found growing in the state under a wide variety of conditions. A prairie species *P. pilosa* L. grows in full sunlight of prairie environments and develops a deeper colored flower. Some species were grown in flower gardens and have escaped to the wild. The common sweet William of gardens is a member of the pink family, not of the phlox family. The phlox family is most readily recognized by checking for the typical three branches to the style (tube which extends from the ovary).

In early medicine, leaves of some phlox species were made into a tea and used to treat eczema and to "purify the blood." A tea of boiled roots was once thought useful in treating venereal disease. Any other medicinal or food uses by Indians or pioneers are not known.   *...photograph by Marvin Dove*

Wild geranium: *Geranium maculatum* L.

Other common names: alum bloom, alum root, American kimo root, chocolate flower, crane bill, crowfoot, culver root, dove's foot, love knot, pigeon foot, red robin, rock weed, sailor's knot, shame face.

Geranium: from Greek for "heron" or "crane", probably because the seed capusle resembles the beak of a bird.

Maculatum: from Latin for "spotted" referring to the brown and white spots often seen on the leaves. At least one other species is also found, but with less frequency.

Geranium family: *Geraniaceae.*

Found throughout the state in rich moist open woodlands, often in thick stands. Blooms April to June.

The erect stem, to 2 feet tall, is hairy and sometimes branched. Large leaves, to 6 inches across, are essentially round but so deeply cut into three to five lobes that the roundish shape tends to escape notice. Margins of each lobe have prominent teeth. Basal leaves are on long petioles. Leaves along the stem are opposite and often show brown and white spots. Upper leaves have fewer lobes and shorter petioles. Branching flower stems may also have a leaf on a short petiole.

The perennial rootstock is a coarse, thick and knobby rhizome.

The flower, to 1½ inch across, varies in color – mostly shades of a rose-lavender with delicate veining. The few flowers, usually solitary, may appear in loose open clusters at the ends of weak hairy flower stalks, usually one or 2 inches long.

The five rounded petals form a saucer-shaped flower. They are somewhat woolly at their bases. Five green sepals are smaller, narrower, and pointed.

The fruit is an erect capsule resembling a bird's beak perhaps 1½ inch long. The capsule is in five parts, each containing a single seed. It splits lengthwise throwing seeds forcefully away from the plant.

Chippewa Indians dried and powdered the roots to provide a treatment for sore mouth, especially in children. Along with the Ottawa tribe, they also made a tea of the plant for treating diarrhea.

Meskwaki brewed a sort of root tea for toothache and neuralgia. They also made a poultice of pounded roots for hemorrhoids. Boiling the base of the plant produced a "tea" for drinking and a poultice for burns.

Pioneers used the wild geranium as an astringent and as a diarrhea treatment, especially for infants and people with delicate stomachs. They also made it into an injection "to strengthen weak rectal or vaginal muscles."

Because of their high tannin content the leaves and roots were collected by some early settlers and used for tanning hides.

The common geranium houseplant is a 'sister under the skin" bred many years ago in Holland. It belongs to the genus *Pelargonium*, native to the Cape of Good Hope in South Africa.

. . . photograph by Alvin F. Bull

Wild strawberry: *Fragaria virginiana* Duchesne.

Other common names: none known.

Fragaria: from the Latin *fraga* meaning generally "having scent" probably in reference to the sweet smelling fruit. This is the classical Latin name for strawberry.

Virginiana: meaning "of Virginia."

Rose family: *Rosaceae.*

Found throughout the state growing in colonies on dry soils of open woodlands, woods edges, meadows and fields. Blooms April to July.

This low ground-hugging plant arises from a spreading fibrous perennial root system. Hairy leaf petioles up to 6 inches long arise from tufts on the runners. Each leaf, one per stem, is divided into three leaflets. Leaflets are sharply toothed broad ovals up to 2 or more inches long.

Sparse open clusters of a few white flowers appear at the ends of hairy erect flower stalks. Individual flowers are usually less than an inch across. They have the five rounded petals and the saucer-like shape typical of the rose family. Flower stalks are shorter than the leaf petioles so the flowers occur below the level of the leaves.

The flowers develop into the familiar scarlet wild strawberry in June and July. The berry is a somewhat irregular globe-shape about one-quarter to two-thirds inch in diameter. Small "seeds" (actually achenes) are imbedded in pits on the surface of the berry. To the botanist the strawberry is not a true berry at all, but a succulent fruit. A true berry is a pulpy fruit with seeds contained in its center.

The less common wood strawberry, *F. vesca* L., is similar except that it is usually taller, carries its flowers at least as high as the leaves, and has seeds (achenes) protruding from the surface of the berry. Another plant called barren strawberry, *Waldsteinia fragarioides* (Michx.) Tratt., appears similar. However, its flowers are yellow and do not develop berries.

Flavor of the berry is sweet and, to most people, even more delicious than garden varieties which are hybrids developed to produce more and larger fruits.. A few people, however, develop an allergic rash from eating wild strawberries.

The wild strawberry served both Indians and pioneers as a favorite food. It was eaten fresh, with shortcake, and as preserves or jam. Indians made a sort of jam to preserve the berries for winter use. Numerous species of wildlife also eat the berries.

Linnaeus believed that eating wild strawberries cured his gout. Early pioneer medicine followed the same thinking. A tea of dried leaves was used as an astringent and to treat diarrhea and dysentary. The dried leaves also make a pleasant beverage. Probably the widest medicinal use was as a fruit syrup to provide a pleasant carrier for medicines. An infusion of strawberry root was once considered a treatment for gonorrhea in England.

Izaak Walton wrote, "Doubtless God could have made a better berry, but doubtless God never did." Finding a bed of ripe wild strawberries can be one of the fringe benefits of going fishing in June or July. *. . . photograph by Donald R. Kurz*

Other common names: bells, clucky, honeysuckle, jack-in-trouser, meeting houses, rock lily.

Aquilegia: probably from Latin *aqua* for "water" and *leger* for "to collect" because fluid does collect in the hollow spurs of the flowers. Some authorities believe it was named after the Latin *aquila* for "eagle" because the flower spur remotely resembles the talons of an eagle.

Canadensis: meaning "of Canada" and applied at a time when Canada extended south to New Orleans and westward.

Buttercup family: *Ranunculaceae.*

Found throughout the state under a wide variety of conditions including loose soil on cliffs and other steep slopes. Blooms April to July.

This openly branching plant grows to 2 feet or more. Its leaves are usually divided into three leaflets, each with three lobes. Leaflets are up to 2 inches across. Lower leaves have long petioles while upper leaves may have none.

Wild columbine is a short-lived perennial with a long coarse tough root system.

Distinctive flowers of scarlet and yellow nod on long individual flower stalks. Flowers, one to 2 inches long, have five petals. Each petal ends in a long red spur tipped with a nectar gland. The spurs are rather straight, not curved or hooked as in some related species. The five sepals appear as yellow "leaflets" attached to the petals. The flower is pollinated by humming birds, moths, and butterflies. Only those pollinators with long tongues can reach the nectar. Bees which attempt to get to the nectar by cutting through the tube find the tube tissue secretes a bitter juice which discourages such efforts.

The seed capsule with five segments is about two-thirds of an inch long. Each segment is tipped with a beak of similar length. Inside are numerous tiny shiny black seeds.

Omaha and Ponca Indian men used to rub pulverized seeds on their palms as a love potion before shaking hands with a loved one. This was also supposed to make them more persuasive when speaking to a council.

A hair wash was made by boiling the entire columbine plant. Roots were boiled and eaten by western Indians in times of famine.

Garden columbines of various colors have been developed from *A. canadensis* L. If seeds of these tamed varieties are allowed to grow, the descendants will revert to the wild form and the horticultural forms will be eliminated from the resulting population.

A large blue-flowered columbine, *A. caerulea* James, is the state flower of Colorado. A stiff fine is levied against anyone caught picking or harming the flower in that state.

. . . photograph by Donald R. Kurz

Violets: *Viola* many species

Other common names: Johnny jumpups.

Viola: the old Latin name for violets.

Species: Numerous species found in the state are highly variable and frequently hybridize. Identification is highly technical.

Violet family: *Violaceae.*

Found throughout the state, usually in colonies, in a wide variety of habitats varying from wet to dry and from woodland to prairie. Violets typically bloom April through June – sometimes all summer.

Violets are low-growing plants, usually under 10 inches tall. Most have a clump of leaves, each on its own petiole arising from a ground-level crown. These have a single showy flower on each of several flower stalks arising from each crown.

Some species have several leaves along a stem which is topped by one or more flowers.

Leaves are usually broad and vary in shape – oval, heart-like, or somewhat triangular. Margins generally have shallow teeth. A few–like the birdsfoot violet–have leaves that are deeply segmented.

Most violets are perennial. Their root systems are somewhat varied, mostly knotty rhizomes with extensive fibrous rootlets. Some send out above ground runners which take root and start new plants.

Showy flowers of the violets have five colorful petals and a spur. The spur varies in prominence, being scarcely noticeable in many species. The petals include an upper pair, two side petals, and a lower one. This lower petal, often longer and larger than the others, serves as a "landing pad" for pollinating insects. This lower petal and sometimes the side petals show prominent colored veining. Petals in a few species are bearded or fringed. Colors are typically shades of purple, sometimes yellow or rarely white. A few are bi-colored. One species, *V. tricolor,* has two upper petals of purple, but the other three petals are of various colors. This is one of the ancestors of the garden pansies.

Some species also have "summer flowers" without petals, or only rudimentary petals which never open, but self-pollinate within the enclosed calyx.

The fruit is a small dry capsule which splits into three parts, each bearing a row of tiny seeds.

In early American medicine, violets were considered to be "blood purifiers."

Dried whole plants of some species were used to treat skin diseases and dysentary. Tea of the birdsfoot violet, *V. pedata* L., was once used for respiratory problems.

In ancient times, a garland of violets was recommended by Pliny, an early Roman naturalist, as a cure for headache caused by a hangover. Other early writers considered violets of value in treating boils, empetigo, ulcers, and even cancer.

Violet leaves are still used in parts of Europe as greens and pot herbs. The flowers have also been boiled in sugar to make an unusual confection.   *...photograph by William Welker*

Other common names: killwort, swallowwort, tetterwort, wartwort.

Chelidonium: from Greek *chelidon* meaning "swallow". According to ancient folklore, the plant tended to flower from the time swallows arrive in the spring until they leave in the fall.

Majus: from Latin meaning "greater."

Poppy family: *Papaveraceae.*

Found throughout the state in shaded, damp woodlands, especially woodland edges, roadsides and steep embankments. Blooms April to September.

A weak but erect and widely branched plant grows to 2 feet tall from a fleshy perennial rootstock. Leaves are thin and smooth but large, to 8 inches long. Each leaf is usually divided into five to seven irregular lobes. Each lobe also may be deeply cut with rounded edges. Leaves are alternate on the stem. Leaf bases are expanded and may partially wrap around the stem. Veins are conspicuous and relatively large. The foliage has a characteristic yellow-green color. Broken plant parts exude a bright orange-yellow juice which produces a durable stain, gives off an upleasant odor, and has a persistent nauseous taste.

Flowers with four yellow petals and two green sepals are up to three-fourths inch across. They grow in loose open clusters on yellowish stems which arise from axils of upper leaves. The fruit is a coarsely roughened capsule about an inch long and containing many shiny smooth but crested seeds.

The widespread but localized occurrence of celandine over the state may tend to indicate the original location of some pioneer doctors. Many of them carried celandine along as they moved into a new area and established their practice. Only in a few places has it spread widely over large areas of woodland.

The plant, probably brought from Europe to the United States by early doctors, contains chelidonine, protopine, chelerythrine, and other alkaloids. The juice was once used to treat warts and corns. It may irritate the skin of some people so children should be discouraged from using the yellow juice in their play.

An ointment of celandine and lard was used for hemorrhoids. In the Middle Ages it was used to treat jaundice following the "doctrine of signatures" which held that plants bearing a esemblance to a body part or disease were useful treatments.

Some early scholars wrote that the plant was named for the swallows because they used the bright orange colored juice to restore sight to their blinded nestlings. Probably because of this, celandine juice was used to treat sore eyes until the middle of the 17th century.

Most common uses in pioneer medicine were as a sedative and as a purgative to cleanse the intestinal tract. It has also been used for toothaches and, in Russia, as a cancer treatment.

. . . photograph by Sylvan T. Runkel

Other common names: ladies' sorrel, sheep grass, sour grass, toad sorrel.

Oxalis: from Greek meaning "sour", referring to the nippy acid flavor from the abundance of oxalic acid found in all parts of the plant.

Species: Three species are common in the state. (Some authorities believe this genus includes the shamrock of Ireland. There is a great deal of disagreement among authorities on the classification of species within this genus.)

Wood sorrel family: *Oxalidaceae.*

Found throughout the state on a wide variety of soils. *O. violacea* L. (violet flowers pictured on left hand page) prefers open rocky woodlands. *O. stricta* L. and *O. dillenii* Jacq. (both with yellow flowers) prefer acid soils and open areas. Blooms April to October.

These low growing plants, often somewhat reclining, have clover-like leaves, but the three leaflets are more heart-shaped. They have a shallow notch on the outer edge and fold along a center crease at night. The leaves may be as much as an inch across.

O. violacea L. (with white to purple flowers) has no stems, only leaf petioles and leafless flower stalks arising from the spreading perennial rootstock. Other species produce bulbs or tubers of several types. Our yellow-flowered species have weak leafy stems which may have many branches. *O. dillenii* Jacq.

seldom has more than three flowers per stem, each on its own slender stalk arising from the same point at the tip of the stem. *O. stricta* L. usually has more than five but less than 10 flowers. Some are borne at the tip of the stem and some on branches off other flowers stalks.

The flowers have five spreading petals, each with a conspicuous notch in the outer edge. Flowers are carried above the level of the leaves. Some species have solitary flowers while others have loose clusters. The petals are sometimes united at their bases. The flowers close at night. They are showy but small, seldom more than a half inch across.

The fruits are small cylindrical capsules which sometimes split open explosively and scatter the tiny seeds about.

All plant parts contain a sour watery juice from which the name sorrel is derived. This gives its foliage the mildly tonic and refreshing quality long known to hikers who pause to chew on a sprig of wood sorrel. It is also used sparingly in salads. Early farmers and gardeners often used this plant as an indicator of "sour" (acid) soil condition.

Leaves, flowers and bulbs were eaten by Indians of various tribes. Indians have used powdered leaves boiled in water to help expel intestinal worms. Species of wood sorrel were also used to reduce fevers and to increase flow of urine.

The whole plant of some species was boiled to make an orange dye. *. . . photograph by Donald R. Kurz*

May apple: *Podophyllum peltatum* L.

Other common names: devil's apple, ground lemon, hog apple, Indian apple, mandrake (no relation the European mandrake), Puck's foot, raccoon berry, vegetable mercury, umbrella plant, wild jalap, yellowberry.

Podophyllum: from Greek meaning generally "foot leaf" probably originating from a still earlier term meaning "duck foot leaf," for the faint resemblance to the leaf shape to a duck's foot.

Peltatum: from Latin meaning "shield-shaped."

Barberry family: *Berberidaceae.*

Found throughout the state on moist soils of open woodlands, usually in colonies. Blooms in May.

This distinctive perennial grows to 18 inches high from a large horizontal rootstock. Large leaves, one or two per plant, top a smooth brittle stem. Each leaf, broadly circular in shape and as much as a foot across, has five to nine deeply cut lobes. Each lobe is veined and coarsely toothed. Single-leafed plants are young and do not flower. The stems of older flowering plants divide toward the top into two branches, each with its own umbrellalike leaf.

A solitary saucer-shaped flower appears on a short stout stalk which arises from the crotch of the stem. Its six to nine waxy white petals combine into an attractive flower that may measure up to 2 inches across. Its odor is considered unpleasant – too sweet – by some. Others may like the smell.

The fruit is a large pulpy berry up to 2 inches long. When fully ripe, it is a greenish yellow color.

Rootstocks, foliage, and green fruits are all poisonous to some degree. Direct contact causes a skin rash for some people.

Ripened fruits lose their toxicity and become edible, either raw or cooked. Pioneers commonly used these fruits to make preserves. They also listed the May apple as "our slowest acting purge, requiring 10 to 24 hours to take effect." It was highly regarded as a treatment for summer diarrhea of children, especially if other remedies had failed. Because this cathartic effect varied from person to person, May apple was usually consumed only in small amounts.

The Potawatomi and Meskwaki tribes favored May apple as a treatment for snakebite. They also brewed it into a tea to treat dropsy. Others included May apple in a mixture of herbs used for syphilis.

May apple was also the ingredient of treatments for urinary, liver, bowel and skin disorders – including warts.

Menomini Indians used May apple as an insecticide. They boiled the entire plant and splashed the resulting liquid over their potato plants to control insects.

Modern medicine is still investigating the May apple. A resin called podophylin derived from the root has proven beneficial for treating certain venereal warts. That same resin may have anti-tumor properties useful in treating some forms of cancer.

. . . photograph by Jim Leachman

Solomon's seal: *Polygonatum biflorum* (Walt.) Ell.

Other common names: conquer John, sealwort.

Polygonatum: from Greek meaning "with many knees", probably referring to the knobby rootstock.

Biflorum: from Latin meaning "two flowered" in reference to the pairs of flowers that hang down from the main stem. Some authorities divide this into three separate species, using *P. communtatum* (Schult.) A. Dietr. and *P. canaliculatum* (Muhl.) Pursh. for the other two.

Lily family: *Liliaceae.*

Found throughout the state, mostly on rich moist soils of woodlands and sometimes in open areas cleared from woodlands. Flowers May and June.

The unbranched stem of Solomon's seal forms a long graceful arch. Highest point of a 6 foot stem may be no more than 3 feet above the ground. This leafy stem is slender and smooth, perhaps somewhat zig-zag toward the end.

The alternate leaves are pointed ovals to 4 inches long and slightly less than half as wide. Prominent linear veins extend from base to tip. The leaves have toothless margins and little if any petiole.

The thick horizontal perennial rootstock has coarse sparse roots extending from its lower side. On the upper side, it bears scars of previous growth. Since only one stem develops per year, the number of scars reveals the age of the plant.

The scars are a somewhat circular impression believed to resemble the ancient seal of King Solomon. Another version has the name derived from the use of crushed roots to "seal" wounds, especially broken bones.

Yellow-green flowers, usually a half to one inch long, hang down in clusters from the leaf axils. They are shaped like elongated bells with lobes on the flared edge. Each flower nods on its own slender flower stalk. The cluster usually has two, but may have three or four, flowers.

The fruits are attractive blue-black berries about the size of a pea. In contrast, false Solomon's seal *Smilacina racemosa* (L.) Desf. has its white flowers and red fruits at the tip of the stem.

The ripe berries, rootstocks, and young shoots were once used for food. Iroquois Indians may even have cultivated Solomon's seal for its roots. Chippewas called the plant "makodjibik" meaning "bear root" and used it for kidney trouble or back pains. For full effect, they felt the medicine must be stored in a bag made of bear paws. Meskwaki and Potawatomi tribes placed a small piece of root on glowing coals to produce fumes for reviving one who had lost consciousness.

Pioneers tried Solomon's seal as a substitute for digitalis in treating heart problems. Preparations of the roots were used to treat hemorrhoids, arthritis, poison ivy, and skin irritations. An extract from the roots was once thought to diminish freckles.

. . . photograph by Marvin Dove.

Sweet cicely: *Osmorhiza longistylis* (Torr.) Britton

Other common names: anise root, sweet anise, sweet jarvil, wild anise, wild licorice.

Osmorhiza: from Greek meaning "sweet smelling root", in reference to the aromatic roots characteristic of this genus. Some botanists still prefer to use the name *Washingtonia* for this genus.

Longistylis: meaning "with long styles", referring to the long narrow tube between the stigma and the ovary. In this species the style is longer than the petals. In a closely related species, the style is shorter.

Parsley family: *Apiaceae (Umbelliferae).*

Found throughout the state on rich moist but well drained soils of cool shady woodlands. Flowers May to June.

The erect green stem, growing to 3½ feet tall, is smooth except for fine hairs at the nodes. Large leaves, as much as a foot across on lower parts of the plant, are divided into three parts and then either further subdivided or deeply toothed to appear somewhat fern-like. The leaves resemble those of the carrot except for being larger and coarser.

The fleshy perennial taproot shaped like a small carrot has a distinct anise or licorice odor.

The plant is sometimes mistaken for the poisonous water hemlock – especially since its stem may develop a dark purplish appearance resembling that of the water hemlock. Sweet cicely does not grow in wet areas preferred by water hemlock. Water hemlock has the odor of parsnips rather than anise.

Tiny white flowers are carried in loose sprays resembling an umbrella in shape. Neither the individual flowers nor the sprays are impressive. The fruits are small, two-pointed, sticky capsules which attach themselves to passing animals – nature's way of insuring distribution of the seeds.

Another species, *O. claytoni* (Michx.) C. B. Clarke, is similar except that its odor is more like parsnips than anise and the entire plant is covered with fine hairs. It's parsnip-like odor is more like the poisonous water hemlock.

The distinct odor and flavor of anise found only in *O. longstylis* (Torr.) Britton has led to many uses. Early settlers used the root as a flavoring for cookies, cakes, and candies. Some chewed the root for its flavor.

Indians made wide use of sweet cicely as a medicine for sore throat. Some tribes also applied a moistened root powder to treat open sores. It is likely that they copied early settlers in using it as a flavoring for some foods.

Another spcies, probably of a different genus in the same family, is the common sweet cicely of England. The resemblance is close enough to cause some disagreement among botanists.

. . . photograph by William Welker

Carrion flower: *Smilax herbacea* L.

Other common names: Jacob's ladder.

Smilax: from Greek meaning "rasping" in reference to the thorns found on most *Smilax* species.

Herbacea: from Latin referring to the non-woody character of the species. Most other members of this genus are woody vines with prominent thorns which give rise to common names such as greenbriar and catbriar.

Lily family: *Liliaceae.*

Found throughout the state on rich soils of woodlands and thickets. Flowers May and June.

Annual vines to 7 feet long grow from perennial tuberous roots. The vines, without the thorns of many *Smilax* species, cling to trees, bushes and fences by means of pairs of tendrils which emerge from leaf axils. The foliage and habitat are quite variable.

Leaves are broadly oval with smooth margins, pointed at the tip, and to 5 inches long. They are alternate along the stem and on petioles usually somewhat shorter than the leaf.

A single plant will produce male or female flowers, but not both. The female plant has clusters of 15 to 80 tiny yellow-green flowers in a ball at the end of a flattened flower stalk usually 4 to 9 inches long. The cluster or ball of flowers is generally from one to 2½ inches in diameter. Perhaps the most distinctive feature of the flowers is the odor of decaying flesh – from which the common name originates. The odor, present only in the flowers, attracts flies and other insects which are necessary for pollination. Male flowers are similar – perhaps slightly larger.

Female flowers produce edible berries that are blue-black when ripe. The tight balls contain up to 80 berries, each perhaps a quarter inch in diameter. A berry holds three to six small seeds. A flower which smells something like a dead rat ends up producing a berry that is edible – another of nature's amazing feats.

Both indians and pioneers used the tuberous rootstocks of carrion flowers as a source of flour. One of the first written accounts of such use was recorded by Captain John Smith in 1626. Meskwaki Indians relished the fruits and called them "asipuni-niminan", their word for coon berries. Omaha and other tribes also ate the berries. Nonspecific medicinal uses by Indians have been reported.

Young shoots resemble asparagus with curling tendrils and have been used as an asparagus substitute.

The berries are a favorite food of birds and animals. Seeds are not digested, so the carrion flower often grows along fences where seeds have been deposited by birds.

Various species of *Smilax* have been used in ornamental plantings. The "smilax" commonly used by florists is an ornamental asparagus, *Asparagus asparagoides* Wight., rather than a true *Smilax*. 			. . . *photograph by W. K. Hollingworth*

Corydalis: *Corydalis aurea* Willd.

Other common names: golden corydalis, slender fumewort.

Corydalis: From Greek meaning "crested lark."

Aurea: from Latin meaning "golden". Other species, all with similar flowers, may be found in Indiana. Small differences in flowers and fruits are often the basis for identifying various species.

Poppy family: *Papaveraceae.*

Found sparingly throughout the state on rocky, sandy or gravelly soils in or near woodlands. *C. aurea* Willd. (golden) prefers less acid soil areas. *C micrantha* A. Gray (tiny-flowered) is rather rare but may be found throughout the state. *C. sempervirens* (L.) Pers. (over-wintering) is a pink-flowered species found mostly to the north. *C. flavula* (Raf.) D.C. (yellow) is rare toward the north, becoming more common to the south. Other species are found, but they are extremely rare. Blooms mostly May and June.

Most plants of this genus are short and delicate. They may be annuals, biennials, or weak perennials. Only under ideal conditions do they form spreading mats interspersed with other spring flowers. Our species are spreading from the base with leafy stems mostly less than 20 inches tall.

Leaves are alternate and finely dissected so that they appear somewhat fern-like. Lower leaves have long petioles. Upper leaves may have short petioles or none at all. Their color is bluish-green similar to that of Dutchman's breeches.

Showy flowers of the corydalis are mostly pale to golden yellow. Two outer petals enclose two inner ones. The upper petals also form a blunt spur which makes the flower appear attached toward its center. In some species, the outer petals also have projections called crests. The flowers grow in small clusters at the top of the plant, usually above the leaves.

The bright yellow flowers of *C. aurea* Willd. are as large as three-fourths inch long. The slightly curved spur is rounded at the end and is about half the length of the flower. The petals show a keel but no crest. Its bracts are conspicuous. The curved finger-like seed pods may be spreading or hanging down along the stem.

C. micrantha A. Gray flowers are a half inch or less in length and without a spur. Their crests may be smooth or sparsely toothed. Flowers and fruits are often no higher than the upper leaves. Its seed capsules are erect.

C. sempervirens (L.) Pers. has pink flowers rather than yellow.

The pale yellow flowers of *C. flavula* (Raf.) D.C. have a short spur and a winged crest which is toothed. Its tiny flowers are about one-fourth inch long. The seed capsules tend to hang down along the stem.

Most, perhaps all, of the species are poisonous – as are the related Dutchman's breeches. Several alkaloids have been isolatd from various species. In early medicine, the corydalis species were considered a general tonic. It also ranks among the many unsuccessful treatments of syphilis.

. . . photograph by Alvin Bull

Poison Ivy: *Rhus radicans* L.

Other common names: climbing sumac, markweed, mercury, three-leaved ivy.

Rhus: from Greek, the ancient name for this species. (Some authories list the poisonous species in a separate genus, *Toxicodendron.*)

Radicans: from Latin for "rooting", because the stems send out rootlets.

Sumac family: *Anacardiaceae.*

Found widely through the state under a wide range of conditions. Blooms May and June – but this plant is to be avoided at all times.

Poison ivy may take the varied forms of bush, small tree, or vine which spreads like ground cover and climbs on fences, bushes, and trees. This perennial plant has a woody stem ranging from twig size to 4 inches or more in diameter. Its root system is shallow but widely spreading.

Leaves on long petioles are alternate, divided into tell-tale clusters of three leaflets. Leaflets are often shiny or waxy above, light and somewhat fuzzy underneath. Size, shape, and color of leaflets are varied. Margins may be smooth but usually show some shallow notching. Color varies from dark to light green, sometimes tinted with red. They turn brilliant red in the fall – attractive enough to be picked for floral arrangements by the unsuspecting.

Tiny inconspicuous green flowers are about one-sixth of an inch across. They grow in loose open clusters along a flower stalk. Clusters are often hidden by the leaves. The fruit is berry-like, creamy white, and about one-fourth inch in diameter. Berries may persist through the winter unless eaten by birds, which assist in spreading the seeds.

Poison ivy rates mention with the state's wild flowers because it is so wide spread and because all parts of the plant are poisonous. Degree of immunity varies among people, and even month by month for individual persons. People have even been seriously affected by smoke given off from burning poison ivy plants.

The poison causes inflamation with spreading blisters and scabs, usually beginning 12 to 24 hours following exposure. Wash as soon as possible after touching the plant, preferably with an alcohol solution to remove the slightly volatile oil which causes the problem.

Poison ivy need not be feared – just avoided.

Meskwaki Indians named the plant "tatapakwi", meaning "climbs trees" – and considered it "dangerous medicine" to be used only by the most skilled medicine men. Among the infrequent uses was fresh root pounded to a pulp and applied as a poultice to open a swollen wound. More recent medicine men report that the benefits were not worth the risk.

Early settlers introduced the plant to England where it was tried as a treatment for obstinate skin eruptions, palsy, paralysis, and rheumatish.　　　*...photograph by Kitty Kohout*

Wild grape: *Vitis riparia* Michx.

Other common names: frost grape, riverbank grape.

Vitis: from Latin meaning "grape."

Riparia: from Latin meaning generally "living on the bank of a river or lake." Other less common species are also found in the state.

Grape family: *Vitaceae.*

Found throughout the state on moist but well drained soils, most often along streams or roadsides. Flowers in May and June.

This vigorous climbing woody vine grows to an inch or more in diameter and climbs to great heights. The grayish-brown bark of older stems scales off in long strips. Young branches are green or dull red. Numerous coiling tendrils provide the ability to climb.

The perennial root system is extensive.

Large leaves, 6 to 8 inches long and nearly as wide, are alternate along the stem on long petioles. Margins are toothed and have three to seven shallow lobes. The center lobe is longer than the others.

Some similar, but less common, species are also found in the state.

Tiny light green flowers are borne in loose clusters along a flower stalk arising from axils of upper leaves. Although otherwise inconspicuous, the flowers are pleasantly fragrant and may perfume the air where grapes are abundant.

Clusters of fruit ripen to a frosty blue-black color about the time of first frost. They have a characteristic "bloom" as if dusted with a fine white powder. Individual fruits containing two to four seeds may be as much as a half inch in diameter under favorable conditions.

Fruits of wild grapes were well known to Indians who gathered great quantities and dried them for winter use. Pioneers found the fruits especially delicious in jams and jellies. Of course, both ate them fresh from the vine.

The Cherokees boiled wild grape and geranium root to produce a rinse for the mouths of children affected by thrush. The geranium root with its astringent properties was probably the active ingredient since other tribes and early settlers used it without the addition of grape.

Fresh juice of the grape was used by the Menomini to wash wild rice hulls from the eyes during harvest and threshing.

Both Indians and pioneers once provided new mothers with a tea brewed from wild grape twigs soon after childbirth.

Meskwaki children used a similar tea to ease the pain after they had been tricked into tasting "Indian turnip" (*Arisaema triphyllum* Torr.).

Juice from the vine was thought to be a good tonic for the stomach and intestines. In early times it was even mentioned as a cure for insanity.

Of course, wild grapes are an important food for wildlife – deer, raccoon, fox, rabbits, skunks, turkeys, doves, quail, and others.

. . . photograph by Sylvan T. Runkel

Wild sarsaparilla: *Aralia nudicalis* L.

Other common names: false sarsaparilla, rabbit root, shot bush, small spikenard, wild licorice.

Aralia: The original specimen sent by a Quebec physician to Europe was listed by its French Canadian name "Aralie" which probably came from the Iroquois Indian language.

Nudicaulis: from Latin meaning "naked stem."

Ginseng family: *Araliaceae.*

Found mostly on poorer, relatively dry and well drained soils, especially in the northern part of the state. Blooms May to June.

A single leaf petiole seems to grow to about 18 inches tall directly from the root, but it actually arises from a short ground-level stem. The leaf divides into three sections, each with three to five slender-stalked oval leaflets. Leaflets may be up to 5 inches long and have toothed margins.

New plants arise from the long fleshy perennial rootstock, so plants often appear in small colonies. The root has a distinct and pleasing fragrance.

Tiny greenish flowers to one-eighth inch across form loose ball-shaped clusters. These clusters are 2 or 3 inches in diameter. These balls of 12 to 30 flowers each top a separate stalk that is shorter than the leaf petiole. As a result, the inconspicuous flower clusters are often nearly hidden beneath the leaves. The lone flower stalk is topped with two to seven of these flower clusters. The most common number of clusters (technically umbels) on a plant is three. Individual flowers have five petals, each curved back at its tip. The flowers are tiny, usually measuring only about one-eighth inch across.

The fruit is a cluster of dark purple berries usually less than one-quarter inch in diameter and resembling bird shot. Each berry contains five seeds.

Indians made much use of the plant. The Crees were said to have considered the plant to be a cure for syphilis. Others powered the root and applied it as a poultice to infected sores. Plains tribes used it widely as a diuretic and stimulant. Meskwaki Indians mixed it with other herbs for many internal and respiratory troubles.

Early pioneers used wild sarsaparilla to treat fevers, chills, and afflictions of the throat and chest. They also made an aromatic tonic considered to be a gentle stimulant.

The aromatic roots have long served as an ingredient in root beer. And while they made a passable tea, they were not the source of the once-popular sarsaparilla drink.

Indians are said to have existed on sarsaparilla roots while on forced marches.   ... *photograph by LeRoy Pratt*

Other common names: climbing bittersweet, climbing orange root, fever twig, fever twitch, staff vine, waxwork.

Celastrus: from Greek for a kind of evergreen plant.

Scandens: from Latin for "climbing" referring to the general growth habit of the species.

Staff tree family: *Celastraceae.*

Found throughout the state, especially on rich well-drained soils of woodlands. Blooms mostly in June.

This sturdy perennial vine may produce twining woody stems 30 feet or longer and an inch or more thick at the base. It climbs by winding itself around other vegetation – sometimes even around its own stems. The twisting stems may kill saplings by restricting further growth. Twigs are yellowish-green to brown and often winterkill at the tips.

The alternate leaves are broadly oval, frequently somewhat pointed at the tip. Leaves, to 4 inches long and half as broad, are on petioles as much as three-fourths inch long. Margins may be smooth, uneven, or with fine shallow teeth.

Tiny inconspicuous flowers without scent are borne at the tips of branches in loose terminal clusters to 4 inches long. Close examination of individual flowers shows five greenish-white petals that are oblong in shape. Most often, male and female flowers are on separate plants.

Bittersweet is noted for its colorful fruits rather than its flowers. Individual fruits are pea-sized, nearly round, finely wrinkled, and brilliant orange. They split into three parts to disclose a scarlet berry inside. The berry has three sections. Each section contains one or two shiny brown seeds. Clusters of fruits, gathered before frost and dried, make long lasting and colorful decorations.

Bark from the bittersweet root was used by Indians and pioneers to induce vomiting, to treat veneral disease, as a diuretic, and for symptoms of tuberulosis. It was also mixed with animal fat to produce a salve for skin cancers, tumors, burns, and swellings. Berries were sometimes used to treat stomach troubles. The Menomini tribe mixed bittersweet with other plants for relief from pains during childbirth.

Bittersweet is listed as a poisonous plant in some publications – perhaps because related European species have caused poisoning of horses and people. Although the American bittersweet is suspect, cases of actual poisoning are not known. The inner bark and twigs were considered poisonous by some Indianas, but others boiled them for an emergency food supply. An extract from the bark of the root and the stem provided an insecticide for early settlers. Just how effective it was for this purpose is not known.

The berries are also eaten by birds. Undigested seeds are widely scattered by their droppings, especially along fencerows.

. . . photograph by Bruce Plum

False Solomon's seal: *Smilacina racemosa* (L.) Desf.

Other common names: golden seal, Job's tears, Solomon's plume, treacle berry, wild spikenard, zigzag.

Smilacina: from Greek meaning "small and thorny" – misnamed in the sense that it has no thorns although the leaves are similar to those of the thorny *Smilax* species.

Racemosa: from Latin meaning "having a raceme" referring to flowers borne in a raceme – along the end of the main stem on short individual flower stalks.

Lily family: *Liliaceae.*

Found throughout the state in cool woodlands where there is plenty of moisture. Blooms May to July.

The stiffly arching stem and leaves resemble those of the true Solomon's seal. The stems, to a height of 3 feet, may be slightly angled where leaves join the stem. The elongated thick fleshy knotty rootstock of this perennial is a brownish color.

Firm, spreading leaves, often a dozen or more, are alternate along the stem. They are oval, pointed toward the tip, and 3 to 6 inches long, one to 3 inches wide. They have smooth margins, prominent parallel veins and extremely short petioles.

Tiny creamy white star-shaped fowers with six petals are borne in a branched cluster at the end of the stem. Clusters are to 4 inches long.

The edible fruits are ruby red berries about one-fourth inch across, often speckled with brown or purple, and having a sort of bitter-sweet taste. This flavor, said by some early settlers to resemble that of treacle or molasses, is the origin of one common name. In contrast, the true Solomon's seal has pairs of white flowers – and later dark blue berries – drooping on slender stalks which arise from leaf axils.

False Solomon's seal was widely used by Indians. The Ojibwa tribe prepared the rootstocks in a manner similar to potatoes – after soaking in ashes mixed with water to get rid of a bitter taste. The Blackfoot Indians used a powder prepared from dried roots to arrest bleeding. A Nevada tribe once considered a tea of the leaves to function as a contraceptive. Meskwaki and Prairie Potawatomi tribes prepared a smudge of false Solomon's seal to hush a crying child, to treat convulsions or insanity, or to produce other tranquilizing effects. It was also used by some Indian medicine men when they wanted to "do tricks or cast spells."

Early settlers used the plant in home remedies for headache and sore throat. Sometimes they referred to the fruit as scurvy berries – and probably ate it as a treatment or preventive. They sometimes used young shoots as a substitute for asparagus. In early folklore, some even thought false Solomon's seal could be used as a preventive for human plague and for hog cholera.

Another species, starry false solomon's seal, *S. stellata* (L.) Desf., is a similar but smaller plant. The flowers are fewer but larger. They also occur in a single cluster at the end of the stem. The berries are nearly black or with black stripes when ripe, instead of red. *...photograph by Lloyd Huff*

Yellow ladyslipper: *Cypripedium calceolus* L.

Other common names: ducks, golden slipper, Indian shoe, moccasin flower, nerve root, Noah's ark, pouch flower, Venus shoe, whippoorwill shoe.

Cypripedium: an incorrectly Latinized version of the ancient Greek word *Kypris* (the counterpart of Venus, mythological goddess of love) and *pedilon* meaning "shoe." Sometimes referred to as *Cypripedilium*.

Calceolus: from Latin for "a small shoe."

Orchid family: *Orchidaceae*.

Found, now rarely, throughout the state on rich soils of moist to wet woods and swamps that are undisturbed by livestock. A delicate balance between certain fungi in the soil and this species make transplanting mostly unsuccessful. Blooms May to July.

Simple erect stems, often in clumps, grow to 2 feet tall. Three to five alternate leaves sheath the stem with their bases. The leaves, to 6 inches long and half as wide, have smooth margins, pointed tips, and numerous parallel veins. Both leaves and stems are somewhat hairy. The glandular hairs give off a fatty acid that may cause a rash similar to poison ivy on some people.

The perennial root system is a central rhizome branching into twisted roots with many fibrous rootlets.

The showy blossoms feature a hollow inflated lip or "slipper" which is actually a specialized petal. It's color is a waxy lemon yellow. Its opening is incurved and sometimes surrounded by purplish spots. Two spreading lateral petals are purplish brown strap-like spirals, slightly longer than the lip. The lip usually ranges from three-fourths to 2 inches long. Another species or variety with smaller flowers is also found.

One sepal, purplish brown and broadly lance-shaped, rises above the lip. The other two sepals are united under the lip. Each plant generally has one or two flowers.

The fruit is a three-celled capsule containing many minute seeds.

North American Indians used the powdered root as a sedative, tranquilizer, and pain reliever. Pioneers soon adopted the practice.

A long list of other uses are related, including treatment of toothache, nervous depression, neuralgia, hysteria, epilepsy, insomnia, intermittent fevers, and alcoholic delirium tremens. Typical treatment was about a teaspoon of powdered root mixed with about a cup of sugar water.

The Menomini and Ojibwa tribes favored such a root "tea" for "female problems" and for easing the pains of childbirth.

A closely related species, now rare in the state, is the pink-flowered whippoorwill moccasin (*C. acaule* Ait.). It was part of a love potion favored by the Meskwaki tribe.

. . . photograph by Mrs. Arthur Wicks

Yellow pimpernel: *Taenidia integerrima* (L.) Drude.

Other common names: golden alexander (also applied to another plant).

Taenidia: from the Greek *tainidion* meaning "a small band" referring to the ribs on the seeds.

Integerrima: from Latin for "most entire" referring to the smooth margins of leaflets.

Parsley family: *Apiaceae (Umbelliferae).*

Found infrequently throughout the state in dry open woodlands, rocky hillsides, sandy areas, thickets, and prairies. Blooms May to July.

The smooth slender erect stem of this delicate perennial often has a whitish powdered appearance. It is usually simple but may be slightly branched. Height of this graceful plant is usually one to 3 feet.

The alternate leaves are divided into two or three segments. Each segment has three to five leaflets. Leaflets are slender ovals one half to one inch long. While these leaflets are not toothed, they may have thumb-like projections. The lower leaves are on longer petioles. A sheath at the base of the leaf petiole clasps the stem. The leaflets have a whitish powdery appearance.

The perennial root system of this species is more spreading and fibrous rather than the usual deep tap root of the parsley family.

Tiny yellow flower heads form a loose umbrella-shaped cluster to 3 inches across. The cluster usually contains 10 to 20 stalks, each tipped with its own small head of flowers. The minute individual fowers are less than one-eighth inch across. Each has five yellow petals which curve inward at their tips.

Each fruit has two tiny seeds, less than one-eighth of an inch long, adjoining to form an oval. The touching surfaces are slightly concave. Four tiny ribs run lengthwise of the fruit.

The yellow pimpernel plant resembles the other golden alexander (*Zizia aurea* W.B.J. Koch), but leaflets of the latter have toothed margins. Meadow parsnip and wild parsnip are also similar but much coarser plants.

In early folk medicine, a tea of yellow pimpernel roots was given for lung trouble. Both Indians and pioneers mixed pimpernel root with other medicines to impart a pleasant aroma. The Meskwaki even used it as a seasoning agent for some of their foods. *. . . photograph by W. K. Hollingsworth*

Other common names: mayflower, pentstemon, pride-of-the-mountain.

Penstemon: from Greek meaning "five stamens." This genus is sometimes referred to as *Pentstemon.*

Species: Of about 300 species found in North America, probably less than a dozen are found in the state. Differences are often minor, requiring expert techical knowledge for positive identification.

Snapdragon family: *Scrophulariaceae.*

Found throughout the state, mostly in open woodlands and edges of woodlands. Flowers appear May to July.

The various species grow one to 4 feet tall with erect stems that are somewhat hairy. Sometimes several stems arise from a single perennial crown. Leaves are opposite, without petioles, and often clasping the stem. They are typically lance shaped, but relative width varies with the species. Leaf margins of most are toothed, sometimes with considerable space between the teeth.

Multiple clusters of flowers form a loose head along the tops of the main stems. Each cluster has its own stalk, with stalks arising in pairs from upper leaf axils. Individual flowers are tubular and two-lipped like those of the snapdragon. The upper lip tends to be more erect with two spreading lobes. The lower lip has three lobes. Color may be pink, lavender, or white depending upon the species.

One of the five stamens is sterile and does not produce pollen. It is often modified into a hairy or bearded tongue and probably attracts insects.

P. calycosus Small – smooth beard tongue – wooded slopes and woodland edges throught the state. Flowers are usually purplish and measure no more than 1¼ inches long.

P. hirsutus (L.) Willd. – eastern penstemon – dry banks and rocky bluffs throughout the state. Flowers are usually purplish and less than an inch long.

P. digitalis (Sweet) Nutt. – foxglove beardtongue – open woods and meadows throughout the state. White flowers are no more than 1¼ inches long.

P. pallidus Small. – pale beard tongue – woodlands, open areas and roadsides, common in southern counties but less frequent elsewhere. White to purple flowers are about three-fourths inch long.

P. tubiflorus Nutt. – funnel-form beardtongue – rare but throughout the state, preferring open woodlands. Flowers, usually white to purplish in color, are less than one inch long.

Indian tribes made several uses of *P. pallidus* Small. For toothache, the root was chewed and pulp placed in the painful cavity. The root was also used to treat rattlesnake bite.

The more showy species of penstemon are used in flower gardens.

. . . photograph by Dean Roosa.

Virginia waterleaf: *Hydrophyllum virginianum* L.

Other common names: brook flower, John's cabbage.

Hydrophyllum: from Greek *hydro* for "water" and *phyllon* for "leaf", in reference to the water-marked appearance of the leaves.

Virginianum: indicating that it was first studied in Virginia. Another species, *H. appendiculatum*, is known as appendaged waterleaf. Two other species are less common.

Waterleaf family: *Hydrophyllaceae.*

Found throughout the state, often in extensive colonies, on rich moist soils of shady woods. Appendaged waterleaf is less common but widespread in local areas. Blooms May to July.

The stiff erect grooved stem of Virginia waterleaf grows one to 3 feet tall. It tends to be smoothish while that of appendaged waterleaf is hairy. Stems of both species are usually single but may be branched.

Virginia waterleaf has an extensive scaly perennial rootstock. Appendaged waterleaf may be biennial.

The numerous large hairy leaves are broadly triangular in shape and alternate along the stem. They are lobed almost to the mid-ribs into five to seven leaflets. Even some of these leaflets may be further lobed. The basal pair of leaflets is usually two-lobed while the upper three leaflets are usually three-lobed. The total leaf is large – as much as 10 inches long.

Veins of these coarse leaves are prominent and margins are irregularly toothed. Upper leaves tend to have shorter petioles, fewer segments or leaflets, and smaller size. Petioles of lower-leaves are often longer than the leaflets themselves.

The surface of the leaves is often marked as if stained by water. This marking remains even after the foliage is dead.

Leaves of appendaged waterleaf are less deeply cut and resemble maple leaves in general outline.

Tight irregular clusters of white to lavender, sometimes purple, flowers are held above the leaves on the erect flower stem. Individual flowers, to one half inch long, are shaped as a tiny fluted bell. The five petals which join toward their bases have bluntly pointed tips. Close examination shows a linear appendage inside each lobe. Five stamens protrude from the "bell", giving the flowerhead a rather hairy appearance. Stamens of the appendaged waterleaf are not so prominently protruding.

The fruit of both species is a dry pea-sized capsule containing one or two thick spherical seeds in each of two sections.

Iroquois, and perhaps other Indian tribes, used the tender young leaves of Virginia waterleaf as greens. In early pioneer medical practice, the plant was listed as an astringent.

Further uses for food or medicine are not known.

. . . photograph by LeRoy Pratt

Poison sumac: *Rhus vernix* L.

Other common names: poison ash, poison dogwood, poison tree, poisonwood, swamp sumac, thunderwood.

Rhus: from Greek, the ancient name for the genus. (Some authorities list the poisonous species in a separate genus, *Toxicodendron*).

Vernix: from Latin for "varnish", probably because processed juice of some sumac species provides a base for lacquers.

Sumac Family: *Anacardiaceae.*

Found mostly in swampy or boggy areas mostly in the northern part of Indiana; less common in the south. Blooms May to July – but this plant is to be avoided at all times.

Poison sumac is included here only to make flower lovers aware of its poisonous qualities which resemble poison ivy, though perhaps more severe. This perennial grows as a coarse open shrub or small tree with gray smoothish bark. The erect trunk, to 6 inches across and 25 feet tall, divides toward the top into coarse branches and twigs showing prominent buds.

The alternate leaves are typical of sumac. (They also resemble the compound leaves of ash trees.) Seven to 13 oval to pointed leaflets are arranged on opposite sides of a common petiole which may be 15 inches long. Leaflets are attached at about 45 degree angles, pointing toward the tips. Individual leaflets may be up to 4 inches long and 1½ inches wide, generally thin oval in shape but pointed at the tip. Margins are without teeth.

Tiny inconspicuous greenish flowers form loose open clusters to 8 inches long on stalks drooping from leaf axils. Individual flowers are less than one-eighth inch across. The grayish white berry-like fruits about the size of a small pea hang in loose clusters and often persist through the winter.

Foliage of poison sumac is among the most beautiful of the woods in autumn – tempting to pick for home decorating. Any sumac growing in wet or swampy areas should be avoided. Non-poisonous sumac prefers dry areas and has fruits of reddish to purplish color.

Symptoms from direct contact with poison sumac are similar to those of poison ivy – inflamation with spreading blisters and scabs. They tend to be more severe than those from poison ivy.

Some people, although relatively few, have also proven allergic to both ordinary smooth sumac and staghorn sumac.

Juice of the plant boiled in water to evaporate the volatile oil results in a fluid "varnish" which provides a permanent glossy black coating. As such, it was once used for finishing boots and shoes – until the toxic side effects were traced.

In *American Medicinal Plants* author Charles F. Millspaugh explains lack of medicinal uses in these words, "The poisonous nature of this species has precluded its use in domestic and previous practice . . . very few persons who understand the plant will even approach its vicinity unless compelled by circumstances to do so."

Poison sumac is related to the lacquer trees of Asia. Interestingly, the cashew nut is a member of the same family.

. . . photograph by John Kohout

Goatsbeard: *Aruncus dioicus* (Walt.) Fern.

Other common names: wild spirea.

Aruncus: from Greek, the original name given this genus by Pliny the Elder, early Roman naturalist and writer. Meaning of the word is lost in antiquity.

Dioicus: from Greek meaning "two houses" referring to the bearing of male and female parts on separate plants.

Rose family: *Rosaceae.*

Found, now rarely in the state, in moist woods and shady places – especially along bluffs. Grows mostly in southern counties and farther south. Flowers May to July.

This showy perennial grows more or less erect to as much as 7 feet tall. Its few large leaves are divided into paired leaflets along a central petiole, plus one at the end. Usually there are five to seven segments per leaf. There may be further division of the segments of the lower leaves. Each final division is a slender pointed oval with toothed margins – resembling a large rose leaf 2 to 5 inches long.

A variety, or at least a variation of this species, has thicker foliage, grayer color, and soft hairs on the underside of the leaves.

Fragrant masses of tiny (about one-sixteenth inch across) creamy white flowers rise above the leaves in magnificent plume-like clusters. Close examination reveals five petals and five sepals. Male flowers have numerous stamens while female flowers usually have three pistils. The male and female flowers are borne on separate plants. Both sexes of flowers grow in slender flower spikes, usually up to 3 inches long. The individual spikes protrude from the main flower stem at varying angles producing an overall cluster perhaps 3 feet long. The result is a somewhat scraggly but unusual and striking beauty – perhaps sufficiently reminiscent of a goat's beard to have given rise to the common name.

The female flowers mature into small fruit pods which later split to release tiny seeds. The seeds, usually two per flower, are vigorous and germinate readily and provide the major means of propogation..

A similar plant, the cultivated astilbe, is sometimes called false goatsbeard. Astilbe flowers generally have 10 stamens and two pistils.

Goatsbeard is also a common name for an entirely different plant found along roadsides and in waste places. Sometimes known as wild salsify or oysterplant, this plant has yellow or purple daisy-like heads.

No medical or food uses of the *Aruncus* genus by Indians or pioneers are known. This unusual species was, and still is, included in flower gardens for its showy flowers and for its handsome much-divided foliage.   *. . .photograph by John Schwegman*

False coffee: *Triosteum perfoliatum* L.

Other common names: fever root, feverwort, horse gentian, horse ginseng, tinker's weed, white ginseng, white gentian, wild coffee, wild ipecac, wood ipecac.

Triosteum: from Greek meaning "three bones" (originally *Triosteosperum* meaning three bony seeds), referring to three hard seeds found in each fruit.

Perfoliatum: from Latin meaning "through the leaf" – actually two opposite leaves joined together around the stem.

Honeysuckle family: *Caprifoliaceae.*

Found throughout the state on well drained soils of dry open woods, especially in thickets on slopes with limestone outcrops. Flowers May to July.

A single erect stem, stoutish and quite leafy, grows 3 to 4 feet tall. The stem is smooth with fine glandular hairs on the upper portion. It's strictly herbaceous, not woody, even though a member of the honeysuckle family. This perennial has a coarse fibrous root system.

The dark green and thickish leaves of false coffee are opposite, often joined together around the stem. The are broadly lance-shaped, to 9 inches long and half as wide, and pointed at the tip. Some leaves toward the middle of the plant tend to be more fiddle-shaped. The margins are smooth. The surfaces have a soft velvety down underneath and are hairy above.

Clusters of erect flowers grow on short stalks in the axils of the upper leaves. These clusters contain mostly three or four flowers, sometimes as many as eight. Individual flowers are tubular or bellshaped, to three-fourths inch long. They are reddish-brown at the tip, greenish toward the base. Each flower has five overlapping petals.

Fruits resemble little oranges, perhaps slightly egg-shaped, and are covered with fine hairs. A similar species, *T. aurianticum* Bickn., has fruits more red than orange-yellow. The fruits remain in small clusters on the plants through late summer and fall. Each fruit usually contains three hard nutlets.

The colorful berries were gathered in the fall by thrifty Pennsylvania Dutch. The seeds were dried, roasted, and ground as a coffee substitute.

Indians made various uses of the plant. Cherokees and other tribes made a tea for treating fevers. Meskwakis prepared the root for treating a new born infant with a sore head. The root was also used in combination with other herbs to treat snakebite. Onondaga and other tribes mashed and moistened the root for a poultice to apply on painful swellings. Early medical practitioners used the plant for the same purpose. Bark of the root was used to treat constipation.

A preparation of the root was also applied to heal sores and as a general tonic. The common name feverwort comes from treating low fevers. It was also thought to cure rheumatism and hysteria.

. . . photograph by LeRoy G. Pratt

Cattail: *Typha latifolia* L.

Other common names: black cap, blackamoor, bubrush, bugg segg, candlestick, cat-o-nine-tails, flaxtail, great reed mace, marsh beetle, marsh pestle, water torch.

Typha: Ancient Greek name for the genus, said to mean "bog."

Latifolia: from Latin meaning "wide or broad leaf." Actually, the leaves are broad only in relation to a closely related species, *T. angustifolia* L. (Shown in photograph.)

Cattail family: *Typhaceae.*

Found throughout the state on rich wet soils, especially pond and lake margins, swamps, wet ditches, and stream edges. Blooms May through July.

Narrow ribbon-shaped leaves to one inch wide and about 6 feet long are without mid-ribs. They are alternate, clasping the stiff flower stalk near its base. A cross-section of the lower leaves clearly shows air ducts which provide oxygen to the perennial underwater root system. The horizontal branching roots, sometimes 2 to 3 inches thick, may almost form a thin "floor" on the mud near the normal water line.

Each rod-like flower stalk ends in two flowering spikes, one above the other on the same stalk. The upper has male flowers; the lower, female. There is no space between the two spikes in *T. latifolia,* L. but there is in the narrow leaf cattail, *T. angustifolia* L. The latter also has leaves to one half inch wide and narrower heads. *T. (x) glauca* Godr. is a hybrid of these two species and is larger than either parent. Any cattail over 9 feet tall is almost certainly this hybrid. After pollen has been shed, the upper spike dries up and disappears, leaving the familiar cigar-like seed head.

Few plants have been more widely used for food. Young shoots less than 18 inches long were peeled and eaten raw or cooked. Just before blooming and while still enclosed in its sheath or husk, the top spike was steamed or boiled and served like corn on the cob. Pollen was collected by shaking it off into baskets or pots, and used as flour – often in combination with other materials such as corn meal or curly dock seeds. Sometimes it was eaten raw, or cooked with meat or fish.

Some Indians charred the heads in hot coals to get rid of the "down" before eating the seeds.

Sections of rhizomes between leaf clumps were made into flour. At the junction of the rhizome and stalk, is a thickened starchy area sometimes cooked as a potato substitute.

Sometimes the seedhead was broken open and the downy insides used to soothe burns. Chopped root was applied to minor wounds and burns. There are even records of use to treat diarrhea, gonorrhea, and intestinal parasites.

The long tough strap-like leaves were woven into mats for use in the teepee or cabin. Sometimes they were dried and twisted into rope. They have also been used for caulking wooden barrels.

The dried fluffy cotton-like seedheads have been used as insulating material for comforters and as stuffing for pillows.

. . . photograph by Herbert H. Hadow

Calamus: *Acorus calamus* L.

Other common names: beewort, bitter pepper root, calamus root, flag root, myrtle grass, myrtle root, pine root, sea sedge, sweet case, sweet cinnamon, sweet flag, sweet grass, sweet myrtle, sweet sedge, sweet rush.

Acorus: Ancient name, believed to be of Latin origin, for an aromatic plant.

Calamus: Ancient name for a reed.

Arum or calla family: *Araceae.*

Found throughout the state, usually in swamps, marshes, and edges of ponds or streams. While it prefers moist to wet soil, it may also be found in shallow water and on soils that are only slightly moist. Flowers May through July.

This plant grows erect and reed-like to as much as 6 feet tall. A height of 2 to 5 feet is common. The long narrow leaves are sword-shaped, usually less than one inch wide. Each leaf has a stiff mid-rib. The leaves tend to grow in pairs, one sheathing the other at the base.

The aromatic perennial rootstock is long and branching with coarse secondary roots.

Inconspicuous flowers are borne on a small club-like spadix which extends upward at an angle from the erect flowering stem. This flowering stalk (scape) is somewhat triangular in section. Above the spadix it becomes a more leafy – a modified spathe. The flower-bearing spadix is usually 2 to 3 inches long, less than a half inch in diameter. The pattern of tiny greenish yellow diamond shapes is made by the numerous flowers.

The fruit is in the form of small berries. Few seeds are produced by the calamus plant, and few of those seeds produce new plants. New plants arise mostly from the spreading root system.

Meskwaki Indians used the aromatic roots as a physic. They also combined it with other "medicines" as a treatment for burns. The Menomini tribe considered the root to be a cure for stomach cramps. A tea of the root served to treat coughs and tuberculosis.

Pioneers used calamus to treat colic, dyspepsia, and typhoid fever. Some chewed pieces of the dried root to clear the throat.

Candied calamus root was a popular pioneer confection. The root was boiled continuously for a day or two. Then it was cut into small pieces before boiling again for a few minutes in a thick maple or sugar syrup. The inner parts of tender young shoots of calamus have been used to make a tasty spring salad. Some reports indicate that the early Pennsylvania Dutch used calamus root to flavor pickles.

Powdered calamus roots have been used to make sachets and in production of perfume.

Calamus, a town in eastern Iowa, was named for the great numbers of calamus plants once found in that locality before soils were drained for farming.

This is the only species of this genus found growing naturally in United States. An Asiatic species with yellow and green striped leaves is sometimes included in ornamental and landscape plantings.   . . .*photograph by Sylvan T. Runkel*

Wild garlic: *Allium canadense* L.

Other common names: meadow garlic, wild onion, wild shallot.

Allium: Ancient Latin name for garlic.

Canadense: meaning of Canada.

Lily family: *Liliaceae*

Found throughout the state in open woods and thickets, especially bottomlands. Blooms May to July.

A **strong onion-like** odor is characteristic of this entire genus. The leaves are narrow and linear, as much as 1½ feet long. They are flattened on one surface, slightly convex on the other. Unlike some other *Allium* species, the grass-like leaves of wild garlic are not hollow.

The leaves arise from a shallow bulb which seldom measures more than one inch thick. Its outer coat is brown and fibrous; inner layers are white and shiny. This bulb may subdivide as one means of reproducton.

A flower stalk as tall as 2 feet also arises from the bulb. It is topped with a spherical cluster of numerous aerial bulblets. These little whitish to purplish bulbs drop to the ground and take root. Sometimes the bulbs have long slender "tails." The cluster may also have a few flowers on individual stalks extending from the cluster.

The flowers are slender with six white to pinkish petals (and colored sepals) usually separated to their base. Two or three rather broad bracts enclose the base of the flower.

The fruit is a small capsule containing one or two black seeds in each of three segments.

The antiseptic properties of wild garlic – among the most powerful of herbs – were known to both Indians and pioneers. Plant juices were often applied to wounds and burns.

Cheyennes crushed bulbs and stems to form a poultice for boils. Dakotas and Winnebagos found such a poultice to provide relief from bee stings. Some tribes even used this treatment for snakebite.

Both Indians and pioneers sliced the bulbs, cooked them and dissolved maple sugar in the juice to form a cough syrup. This mixture was also considered a good treatment for hives.

Other pioneer medical uses included treatment for fevers, disorders of the blood, lung troubles, internal parasites, skin problems, hemorrhoids, ear ache, rheumatism and arthritis.

Early explorers used wild garlic to control scurvy. When Pere Marquette made his famous journey from Green Bay to the present site of Chicago, wild garlic provided an important part of the food supply.

Some ancient civilizations credited wild garlic and other relatives of the onion with divine properties which imparted strength and courage, fostered love, and removed jealousy.

Ground squirrels and prairie dogs feed on wild garlic bulbs.

. . . photography by Donald R. Kurz

Bunchberry: *Cornus canadensis* L.

Other common names: bunch plum, cracker berry, dwarf cornel.

Cornus: from Latin *cornu* meaning "horn," probably in reference to the hardness of the wood.

Canadensis: meaning generally "of Canada."

Dogwood family: *Cornaceae.*

Found on cool moist humus-rich soils of deep woodlands, sometimes covering extensive areas of the forest floor in northern United States and Canada. Rarely extends south into the northwestern part of the state. Blooms mostly May to July, sometimes to October.

This low plant, usually less than 9 inches tall, arises as single stems from a creeping perennial rootstock. Tough slender cord-like rhizomes provide for the aggressive spreading of the plant when conditions are favorable. It makes an excellent protective ground cover in cool moist woodlands.

The stem appears woody at its base, an indication of its close relationship to the larger shrubs and trees of the dogwood family. Opposite leaves on short petioles form a crowded whorl of four to six unequal leaves toward the top of the stem. Leaves, to 3 inches long, are oval but pointed at the tip. Leaf margins are smooth and veins are conspicuous. A pair of tiny leaves, or scales, occur about midway on the stem.

Each plant appears to carry a single white to greenish white blossom about one inch across. A slender rigid stalk holds this flower about an inch above the whorl of leaves. What appear to be four, sometimes six, petals are actually large whitish bracts. These bracts terminate in a curved blunt point which may collect a drop of dew, adding an unexpected sparkle to the beautiful bunchberry in the morning sunlight. The true flowers are in a tiny inconspicuous greenish-white cluster centered in what appears to be the blossom.

The true flowers produce compact clusters of bright orange-red berries, giving rise to the common name bunchberry. Each berry, about a quarter inch in diameter, contains a two-celled stone with two seeds in each cell. The top of each fruit carries a slight scar from the remains of the flower.

Chippewas, and probably other tribes, ate the berries raw. A root tea was mild enough for treating babies with colic. Some early pioneer medical practitioners held that chewing bunchberry twigs could prevent fevers. A related plant, the beautiful flowering dogwood of more southern areas, served in this way as a substitute for quinine during the Civil war.

The nearly tasteless berries are a favorite of birds. And the plant serves as a browse for deer.

The family name, dogwood, may have come from a brew made from the bark of a European species and used to wash mangy dogs. Or perhaps from the Old English "dagge," meaning dagger or sharp pointed object, since the hardness of the wood favored such uses.

. . . photograph by Sylvan T. Runkel

Blue flag iris: *Iris virginica*, L. variety *shrevei*

Other common names: fleur-de-lis.

Iris: from Greek for "rainbow", perhaps because the species contains flowers of many colors. Iris is the name of the rainbow goddess of Greek mythology.

Virginica: meaning "of Virginia." *Shrevei,* the variety name, honors Ralph Shreve (1927).

Iris family: *Iridaceae.*

Found throughout the state, mostly on wet marshy soils and margins of streams or lakes. It also grows on fertile soils that are well drained. Blooms May to July.

Narrow, sword-shaped leaves to an inch wide and 3 feet long grow mostly erect but with a slight graceful curve. Leaves, with parallel veins, clasp the flower stalk near its base.

Rounded stalks, rising to 2 feet and extending higher than the leaves, are sometimes branched with a showy flower topping each branch. The perennial rootstock is a fleshy horizontal rhizome with fibrous roots. The rhizome has an unpleasant flavor and contains a toxic substance, called iridin. Scars of previous leaf growth show on the rhizome.

The blue-violet flowers resemble the domestic iris with segments generally being more slender and smaller. A single plant often has multiple flowers, sometimes as many as six or more. The down-curving parts shade to lighter colors and show conspicuous veining. The iris appears to have nine petals of varying sizes. In reality, it has three petals, three sepals, and three petal-like branches of the style. These branches of the style arch over the pollen-producing stamens to prevent most self-pollination. The broader sepals have a yellow mid-rib expanding to a bright yellow patch at the base. This patch is distinctly hairy. The petals are narrower and smaller than the showy sepals. The flowers emerge from an "envelope" of two or more papery bracts.

The fruit is a three-lobed oblong capsule to three-fourths inch long. Dull, roundish seeds occur in two rows in each lobe.

Indians used this and related species to treat earache, sore eyes, respiratory problems, liver ailments, and other disorders. To relieve swelling and pain from sores and bruises, both Indians and pioneers pounded the boiled root to a pulp and applied it as a dressing. Early pioneer medical practice sometimes used blue flag to induce vomiting or to "cleanse the intestines."

The orris root used in perfumes and flavorings comes from the root of *Iris florentina,* a related species.

The royal emblem (fleur-de-lis) of France represents the iris, but the exact derivation is obscure. One legend tells that King Clovis was beaten in battle as long as he had three black toads as the emblem on his shield. Queen Clotilde learned from a holy hermit about the powers of a shield said to be as shining as the sun and with irises as an emblem. So she convinced the king to change his emblem from toads to irises, and he was thereafter successful in battle. Some time later, the number of irises in French emblems was standardized at three to represent the Holy Trinity.   *...photograph by Sylvan T. Runkel*

Honeysuckle: *Lonicera (vine)*, Diervilla (bush) species

Other common names: (vine) fly honeysuckle, hairy honeysuckle, trumpet honeysuckle; (bush) northern bush honeysuckle

Lonicera: in honor of a 16th century German botanist and physician, Adam Lonitzer.

Diervilla: in honor of N. Dierville, a 17th century French surgeon.

Species: Native honeysuckles of either vine or bush types are rather rare, but many introductions - especially from Asia - are found.

Honeysuckle family: *Caprifoliaceae.*

Found throughout the state in thickets, woods, and woodland borders - especially on the drier soils. Diervilla species are mostly in northern counties. Flowers May to July.

The honeysuckles are perennial woody vines or bushes. Both have opposite leaves usually one to 3 inches long. Leaves of the vine type have smooth margins. The lower leaves have short petioles, but the upper ones may be perfoliate (joined around the stem so it appears to grow through the leaf). The leaf shape varies - mostly oval with the tip either rounded or pointed.

Leaves of the bush honeysuckle have short petioles and toothed margins. This plant grows shrub-like to about 5 feet.

Flowers of the honeysuckles vary in color and size but have a common distinctive trumpet-like shape. Petals forming the outer flared end of the trumpet may be equal as in *L. sempervirens* L. (shown), but more often are unequal with upper and lower lips. The tubular part may be as much as 2 inches long, but is usually less than an inch. Most are fragrant, but a few species are odorless. The sweet nectar of the flowers is especially attractive to honeybees and hawk moths.

The fruits are mostly red berries, often in pairs. But *D. lonicera* Mill., northern bush honeysuckle, produces a many seeded dry capsule which persists on the plant into winter. The berries are usually bitter, but not toxic. In fact, birds relish the berries and disseminate the seeds widely.

Various honeysuckles had numerous uses in early medicine. Early settlers considered them useful as cathartics, diuretics, and emetics. Indians dried and smoked the trumpet honeysuckle *(L. sempervirens* L.) as a treatment for asthma. Leaves of the plant were chewed and applied to bee stings. Roots of the bush honeysuckle were mixed with other herbs, then boiled and made into a drink to treat for gonorrhea. A root tea was used as a treatment for persons urinating blood - also for those unable to urinate.

The berries, and sometimes root bark, were used to expel worms from pregnant women. The berries were also considered a cure for "interior troubles," lung ailments, and fevers.

Present use of honeysuckle is mostly limited to landscaping, wind breaks, and wild life habitat. The planted species are mostly varieties introduced especially for such purposes.

. . . photograph by Ruth Fagen

Bladder campion: *Silene cucubalus* Wibel.

Other common names: bladder catchfly, cowbell, maiden's tears, white Ben.

Silene: Probably from a mythological Greek god Silenus, the intoxicated foster-father of Bacchus, who was described as being covered with foam and slippery. Others believe the origin of the name lies in the Greek work *sialon* meaning "saliva." Both are in reference to the sticky secretions covering the stems of some campions.

Cucubalus: The origin of this species name is lost in antiquity. It was used in the earliest records which mention this species. A number of other campions or catchflys are found in the state.

Pink family: *Caryophyllaceae.*

Found mostly in the northern two-thirds of the state in open woods, roadsides, and meadows – especially in areas where the vegetation and soils have been recently disturbed. Rare in the southern part of the state. Blooms May through August.

Numerous sparsely branched stems are often reclining or partially so. Their height is commonly less than 18 inches; occasionally, as much as 3 feet. Slender oval leaves, to 2 inches long, taper to pointed tips. They have a blue-green color dulled by a whitish or powdered appearance. Leaf margins are smooth. The leaves are opposite with pairs widely spaced, have no petioles, and are more or less upright along the stem. The perennial root system is a thick fleshy taproot.

Distinctive drooping flowers, usually numerous, appear in loose clusters on branched flower stalks. Each of the five petals is deeply cleft to form two prominent lobes. Petals are usually white, sometimes pale pink, forming a flower about a half inch across. Petals protrude from an inflated calyx from which the origin of the term "bladder" becomes obvious. This bladder, itself about a half inch long, is usually a creamy white color with a conspicuous network of pink to purple veins on its membrane-like cover. It is sometimes described as resembling a tiny melon.

The seedpod is enclosed in a similar cover. The tiny blackish seeds are flattened and circular – and covered with minute knobs.

Young shoots of bladder campion have been used as greens for cooking. Their flavor suggests peas, but with a slightly bitter taste. Although early English authors suggested this plant as a garden vegetable, bladder campion is now regarded as a weed.

Specific use by Indians or early medical practitioners is not known. Perhaps this lack of use stems from the fact that it was introduced from Europe where it found little favor either as food or as medicine.

The common name catchfy refers to the sticky secretion on the stems of some other species. Insects are often trapped in this sticky material.   *. . . photograph by Carol J. Bull*

Four o'clock: *Mirabilis nyctaginea* (Michx.) MacM.

Other common names: umbrellawort.

Mirabilis: from Latin for "wonderful" or "strange." The genus name was once *Admirabilis*, but it was shortened by Linnaeus. (Carolus Linnaeus was a Swedish naturalist and botanist who established the modern method of applying genus and species names to all plants and animals. His book *Species Plantarum* published in 1753 provides the basis for plant classification.)

Nyctaginea: from Greek meaning, indirectly, "nightblooming."

Four o'clock family: *Nyctaginaceae*.

Found throughout the state in dry open woods and woodland edges, but more common in prairies and areas which have been disturbed – such as roadsides. Blooms May through August.

Nearly smooth reddish stems to 5 feet tall are leafy and squarish in cross section. They are profusely forked, especially near the top.

Leaves are opposite with smooth margins and short petioles. They are more or less heart-shaped, to 4 inches long and 3 inches wide. Uppermost leaves are often quite small, appearing more as bracts than as leaves. The root system of this perennial is a thick fleshy taproot.

Pink to purple bell-shaped flowers, to three-eighths inch across, face upward in tight flat-topped terminal clusters. As many as five flowers are seated upon a shallow green cup-shaped platform which is five-lobed and perhaps three-fourths of an inch across. The flower clusters arise from the uppermost forks of the stem branches.

Five showy sepals give the flowers their color since four o'clocks have no true petals. The sepals are joined to form a spreading bell that is fluted or pleated. The flare of the bell has five shallow notches. The flowers open in late afternoon, giving rise to the common name four o'clock.

Fruits are hairy capsules containing tiny hard nutlets – brown, angular, five-ribbed, about one-sixth of an inch long. Membrane-like bracts with prominent veining enlarge during fruiting and persist late in the season.

The common four o'clock of flower gardens, a close relative, is a foreign introduction while the wild four o'clock is a native species.

Navajo Indians used the native four o'clock, dried and powdered together with sheep fat and red ochre, as a treatment for burns. Other tribes pounded the root for a poultice to relieve swellings, sprains, and burns. A brew of the roots was used for controlling internal parasites. For bladder trouble, a tea of roots or of the whole plant was frequent treatment.

Western Indians made many uses of a closely related species – including "inducing visions" when the time for such was considered appropriate. Whether or not early settlers found uses for wild four o'clock plants is not known.

. . . photograph by W. K. Hollingsworth

Indian paint brush: *Castilleja coccinea* (L.) Spreng.

Other common names: bloody warrior, Indian pink, nosebleed, painted cup, prairie fire, red Indian, wickawee.

Castilleja: in honor of an early Spanish botanist, Domingo Castillejo.

Coccinea: from Latin meaning "red."

Snapdragon family: *Scrophulariaceae.*

Found in the northern one-fourth of the state in open woodlands and meadows. Blooms May to August.

Indian paint brush may be annual or biennial. In the biennial form, a basal rosette develops the first year. The basal rosette develops early in the season in the annual form. Leaves of the rosette are broad ovals, sometimes wider near the rounded tip. They are without petioles and range from less than an inch to as much as 2 inches long.

From these basal crowns simple hairy stems grow to 2 feet high. Also without petioles, leaves along these stems are alternate and deeply cleft to produce lobes which appear as fingerlike projections. The total leaf is up to 3 inches long and has three to seven lobes. Veins of these leaves are parallel. Both types of leaves are somewhat hairy.

Roots of Indian paint brush have the ability to penetrate roots of other plants and extract their juices, but the species does not depend on this parasitic tendency.

Flowers of this plant are an inconspicuous greenish-yellow. They are less than an inch long and distinctly two-lipped with each lip deeply cleft. The flowers are nearly hidden in the axils of brightly colored bracts. These floral bracts usually have three lobes, sometimes five. The middle lobe is broader and more rounded at the tip. The bracts are tipped with scarlet, sometimes shading to yellow. They appear on the upper quarter of the stem.

It is from these colorful bracts that Indian paint brush gets its common name. The *Castilleja* genus is extremely complex and provides a source of disagreement among botanists of the western states where species are numerous.

Hopi Indian women prepared a tea of the entire paintbrush plant and drank it as a sort of contraceptive. Navajo Indians steeped the blossoms in hot water to make a treatment for centipede bites.

The Chippewa tribe called the plant a complicated name meaning "Winabojo's grandmother's hair" – probably from the disheveled appearance of the leaves. They used it to treat diseases of women and rheumatism. A tea of the flowers was considered a cure for the common cold.

Uses by early settlers were seldom documented, but fresh blossoms are still considered edible.

. . . photograph by W. K. Hollingsworth

Other common names: lion's beard, old man's whiskers, vase vine.

Clematis: from Greek *klema* meaning "vine branch" in obvious reference to the growth habit of the plant.

Pitcheri: named for its discoverer, Zina Pitcher. A related species, *C. virginiana* L., is found throughout the state. It has white flowers.

Buttercup family: *Ranunculaceae.*

Found on rich soils of woodlands and thickets, generally rare, mostly limited to southern and western counties. Blooms May to August.

This sprawling perennial is a much branched vine 8 to 10 feet long. Slender leaf petioles wrap around branches and twigs of other plants for support. The stem is somewhat six-angled in cross section.

Each compound leaf is made up of three to seven heart-shaped leaflets with pointed tips. The leaflets have smooth margins, but may be lobed or further subdivided into threes. Uppermost and lowest leaves are often without the extra lobes or subdivisions. Leaves are opposite and on long petioles. The root system is fibrous and perennial.

Bell-like flowers to one inch long vary from dull reddish to purple. What appear to be four thick leathery-textured petals are actually sepals. These sepals grow together at their base. Each sepal narrows to a slender tip that flares outward and recurves to give the bell shape. The flower has fine hairs on the outside and appears filled with stamens. A single flower nods on a long slender flower stalk which arises from a leaf axil or the tip of the stem.

C. virginiana L., commonly called virgin's bower, has four petal-like sepals that are white or greenish white. They are narrow elongated ovals in shape, spreading to form a cross with each arm perhaps a half inch long. Many long stamens and pistils arise from the center of the cross. The pistils develop long curving feathery tips to form fluffy balls.

When the fruits of *C. pitcheri* have matured, each small rough seed has a long feathery tail-like appendage giving the seed heads a disheveled appearance. This probably accounts for some of the common names.

In early Indian medicine, roots of the leather flower were sometimes boiled to produce a tea regarded as a general tonic. Some western Indians drank a tea of the bark to reduce fevers. Both Indians and early settlers are said to have chewed the bark for sore throat, colds, and fever.

A liquid from boiled leaves was used to heal sores and cuts of livestock. The leaves and bark were main ingredients of a homemade shampoo. Mashed and moistened seeds made a poultice for burns. Dried and powdered leaves were a soothing dust for syphylitic sores.

Many closely related species may cause dermatitis. So it is likely that leather flower could have the same effect on those who are sensitive to it.   *...photograph by Lloyd Huff*

Nightshade: *Solanum nigrum* L.

Other common names: black nightshade, deadly nightshade, poisonberry.

Solanum: probably from Latin meaning "to quiet down", from the effect of nightshade extract on the nervous system.

Nigrum: from Latin meaning "black." (Includes the *Americanum* designation which some botanists prefer.)

Nightshade family: *Solanaceae.*

Found throughout the state, especially on moist to medium dry soils of open woodlands and woodland borders. It is common around the edge of gardens and house yards. Flowers May to September.

This much branched annual with a smooth green stem may reach 3 feet tall. Alternate leaves on long slender petioles are roughly shaped as an elongated triangle, perhaps as much as 4 inches long. Margins are usually irregularly toothed, but sometimes without teeth. Although dark green, the leaves are thin and nearly translucent. Leaves are typically riddled with insect holes.

Common nightshade flowers are seldom more than a half inch across. They are white, often tinged with purple. Five curved petals join at their bases to form a tiny star. From their center protrudes a yellow "beak" formed by the stamens. Loose clusters of a few flowers droop on slender stalks which arise from the axils of the upper leaves.

Fruits are many-seeded black berries about the size of large peas. They are considered poisonous, especially when green or even partially green. Numerous cases of animals and people being poisoned by nightshade berries have been reported. But specialists do not agree on the degree of toxicity.

Horticulturists have developed a species known as garden huckleberry. It's berries are used in pies and preserves, but only after they are fully ripened.

Another species, *S. dulcamara* L, is a twining plant resembling a vine. It has purple flowers with golden anthers. Fruits are scarlet berries which are usually considered poisonous.

European use of nightshade dates back to the time of Christ. In ancient Dalmatia, the roots were fried in butter and eaten to induce sleep. In Bohemia, the plant was hung over an infant's crib as a hypnotic. In Spain, patients with phthisis (probably an ancient name for tuberculosis) were once buried to their neck in garden loam – and after removal, the body was rubbed with an ointment made from leaves of nightshade. Arabs bruised the leaves and rubbed the pulp on burns.

Other early folk medicine considered nightshade to be a treatment for dropsy, gastritis, nervous disorders, and syphilis.

Indians probably learned from the early settlers how to use nightshade. The Dakota tribe is said to have cultivated nightshade and used the ripe berries for food. Other tribes supposedly used it to treat tuberculosis and internal parasites.

Although many nightshade species are poisonous to some degree, some of our important plants are members of this family. These include white potato, tomato, ground cherry, eggplant and tobacco.

. . . photograph by Alvin F. Bull

Angelica: *Angelica atropurpurea* L.

Other common names: alexanders, archangel, aunt Jericho, bellyache root, dead nettle, great angelica, masterwort, purple-stem angelica, wild celery.

Angelica: named from an early legend which tells of an angel revealing the curative powers of this plant to a monk during one of the plagues which periodically swept Europe during the Middle Ages.

Atropurpurea: from Latin meaning "dark purple" referring to the unusual coloring of the stem.

Parsley family: *Apiaceae (Umbelliferae).*

Found, now rarely, in moist or swampy woodlands of the northern part of the state, mostly along riverbanks. Flowers May to September.

This aromatic plant grows to 6 feet tall with an erect branching stem distinguished by its purple color The smooth stem is hollow but sturdy. It may grow to 1½ inches in diameter. The perennial rootstock is woody and extensive.

Leaves are divided into three parts, each with its own petiole. Each part is further subdivided into three to five segments. Individual segments are coarsely toothed at the margin with veins running to the points of the teeth. Total width of a lower leaf may reach 2 feet. The main petiole of each upper leaf has a swollen basal sheath which tends to wrap part way around the stem.

Tiny white to greenish flowers appear in umbrella-like heads. A head may contain as many as 40 branches and total as much as 8 inches across. These heads are on stalks arising from the upper leaf axils.

The fruit is a tiny rounded oval, somewhat flattened on one side. A thin edge or wing around the oval gives resemblance to a miniature flying saucer.

Leaf stalks of angelica have been eaten like celery, and the flavor is supposed to be similar. Eary settlers boiled parts of the plant in sugar to make a candy – just as they had done in Europe with a closely related species. They also used it as ingredient in cakes. Careful identification was necessary since this plant resembles the deadly water hemlock. (One help in identification – veins of water hemlock leaf run to the notches between teeth, not the points of the teeth as with angelica.)

Roots of angelica (perhaps confused with the poisonous water hemlock) were supposedly used by members of some Canadian Indian tribes to commit suicide. If angelica roots are poisonous, they lose their toxicity when dried because dried roots have been used for emergency food as well as for medicinal purposes – to treat colds, rheumatism, fever, urinary problems, and other disorders. Early European medicine included the belief that the plant could cure alcoholism.

Indians of Arkansas smoked the leaves with tobacco. The Meskwaki tribe boiled the whole plant to make a tea for hayfever. They also used it with a mixture of other plants to prepare a drink to treat a woman with an injured womb.

. . . photograph by James P. Rowan

Daisy fleabane: *Erigeron annuus* (L.) Pers.

Other common names: lace buttons, sweet scabious, tall white weed, whitetop.

Erigeron: from two Greek words meaning "spring" and "old man", referring to the early blooming and to the grayish-white or hoary appearance of some species.

Annuus: from Latin for "yearly," obviously applied since this species is annual.

Daisy family: *Asteraceae (Compositae).*

Found throughout the state in open woodlands, meadows, and roadsides, often growing in extensive colonies. Blooms May to October.

The leafy and stiffly erect stems are usually branched toward the top. They are slightly ridged and somewhat hairy. Maximum height is about 5 feet. The plant is usually annual, sometimes biennial from a basal rosette that starts in late summer.

Wide variation is usual among the leaves. Lower leaves, to 6 inches long and 3 inches wide, are more or less oval in shape with coarse marginal teeth. Their petioles have a distinct margin or wing. Upper leaves are narrower and often without petioles, sometimes without marginal teeth. These upper leaves usually have a few bristly hairs on the margin and on the underside of the mid-rib.

Small daisy-like flowerheads are borne on short flower stalks in clusters at the tips of upper branches. Individual flowerheads about a half inch across have yellow disc centers circled by two or three sets of white rays. These rays, each longer than the diameter of the center disc, may be tinged with purple, sometimes enough to give the rays a slight violet or pinkish color. Rays of the daisy fleabane are the same width along their entire length, unlike the asters.

Also unlike the asters, flower rays are more numerous, blooming starts early in the season, and bracts occur in a single circle around the blossom.

Tiny wedge-shaped seeds, to one-sixteenth inch long, have a tuft of short bristles.

Daisy fleabane derived its common name from a reputation for repelling fleas. It, or a related species, was said to have been used to protect both man and beast during the Middle Ages. Supposedly, flower heads could be dried and placed in a room or near a bed to drive away fleas.

In early medicine, a tea of the blossoms was used as an expectorant. An astringent rectal injection for hemorrhoids was brewed from the entire plant.

Daisy fleabane is one of few American weeds to be naturalized into Europe. Sheep like this weed and may eliminate it from a pasture by choosing it in their grazing.

Varieties of daisy fleabane have been developed for horticultural uses. Their flowers are bright colored – violet, rose, purple, rose, or orange.

. . . photograph by Ruth Fagen

Spatterdock: *Nuphar luteum* (L.) Sibth. and Sm.

Other common names: beaver root, beaver lily, bonnets, bullhead lily, cow lily, dog lily, frog lily, horse lily, yellow pond lily.

Nuphar: the ancient Arabic common name for this genus.

Luteum: from Latin meaning "yellow."

Waterlily family: *Nymphaeaceae.*

Found throughout the state growing on rich bottom muds of shallow waters in lakes, ponds, marshes and slow-moving streams. Blooms May to October.

The flat smooth leaves are broadly oval, sometimes more than 12 inches long and 9 inches wide. Leaf margins are smooth, usually with a deep narrow notch to the petiole attachment. The leaves have more of a mid-rib than other water lilies. They usually float on the water surface, but may be either submerged or held above the water.

The leaf petioles are flattened above with a ridge extending from the mid-rib of the leaf.

The thick spongy perennial rhizome is an irregular cylinder that may be 3 to 4 inches thick and more than 3 feet long.

Bright yellow cup-like flowers to 2 inches high and 3½ inches across may show a greenish or purplish tinge on the outside. Individual petals are small and numerous. The outer sepals are green while the others have bright yellow edges shading to purple or maroon toward their bases. The central disc is green or yellowish.

The mature fruit is a ridged egg-shape perhaps 2 inches long and one inch thick. It contains many seeds resembling popcorn. However, they increase in size without bursting the outer skin when roasted.

Indians ate the root roasted or boiled with meat. The taste is described as bland and sweetish. The seeds were also parched or ground into flour.

Sioux Indians pulverized dried roots into a powder which they used to arrest external bleeding. Pioneers used a root preparation to treat diarrhea and leucorrhea.

Indian women sometimes waded into the water and dislodged the rhizomes with their toes. Sometimes they dove to the bottom in order to reach the roots with their hands. Dislodged roots floated to the surface where they were easily gathered.

An easier method was to raid a supply of roots stored by muskrats as a winter food supply. Some tribes did this as the animals were hunted. Other merely "borrowed" the spatterdock rhizomes and replaced them with food that was more plentiful in order to avoid angering whatever powers looked after the welfare of the muskrats.

The roots provide feed for wildlife – moose, deer, beaver, muskrats, porcupines, and others.   ... *photograph by Robert Read*

Self-heal: *Prunella vulgaris* L.

Other common names: blue curls, carpenter weed, brown-wort, dragon head, heal-all, heart-of-the-earth, hook heal, hook weed, sickle weed, sicklewort, thimble flower.

Prunella: Apparently from German "brunella" which was derived from a word meaning "sore throat" for which the plant was believed to be a cure.

Vulgaris: from Latin meaning "common." This species is sometimes divided into several varieties because of the wide variability of plant characteristics from one locality to another.

Mint family: *Lamiaceae.*

Found throughout the state in moderately moist woodlands and along roadways or in pastures and open areas. Flowers May to frost.

These variable perennial plants grow to 2 feet high, usually less. The stem is sometimes branched, usually erect. It is four-angled, as with other mints, and covered with soft hairs. Roots often start from joints of sprawling branches which touch the ground.

Opposite leaves on petioles are broadly lance-shaped to 4 inches long. The larger leaves are usually toward the top of the plant. Leaf magins are wavy, sometimes with coarse but shallow teeth. Undersides of leaves are often purplish in color.

Flowers are in compact squarish spikes at the ends of branches. Spikes are an inch or more long and a half inch thick when in flower, becoming considerably longer as fruits develop.

Immediately below the flower spike is a pair of small leaves without petioles which appear almost as a "collar." Only a few flowers bloom at a time, giving the spike a continually ragged appearance.

Individual flowers are about a half-inch long, purple or violet but sometimes white. The upper lip is darker in color and forms a hood. The lower lip is three-lobed with outer lobes more pointed. The larger center lobe is rounded and toothed.

Small brown nutlets each contain a single seed. Each is somewhat pear-shaped, slightly flattened and brown with darker lines. Four nutlets occur together in the pod-like calyx.

Self-heal may have been introduced by early migrants from Europe for medicinal purposes. There, it was once considered a treatment for a wide range of maladies – hence the common name. Some authorities consider it native to both the United States and Europe.

It has been widely used by many people in many places – as a gargle for sore throat and to treat hemorrhages, diarrhea, stomach troubles, fever, boils, urinary disorders, liver problems, internal parasites, gas, colic, and female problems.

Apparently, medicinal uses were more common in Europe than in this country. Specific references to its use by Indians and pioneers are few for a plant with so promising a name.

. . . photograph by Donald R. Kurz

Moonseed: *Menispermum canadense* L.

Other common names: maple vine, Texas sarsaparilla, yellow parilla, yellow sarsaparilla.

Menispermum: from Greek *menis* for "moon" and *spermum* for "seed" meaning literally "moonseed."

Canadense: meaning "of Canada."

Moonseed family: *Menispermaceae.*

Found throughout the state on a wide range of woodland soil conditions. Blooms June and July.

This deep rooted perennial is a woody climber with a slender stem up to 12 feet long. It may even spiral around erect woody plants, eventually strangling them. The stem is mostly smooth, sometimes slightly fuzzy.

The alternate leaves are large, 5 to 10 inches wide, and quite variable in shape. Most have five to seven shallow lobes, but some are nearly round with a somewhat pointed tip. Margins are without teeth. The leaf is attached to its petiole on the underside and just slightly away from the margin. The leaves and vine may be confused with wild grapes, but grape leaves usually have toothed margins and a deeper indentation where the petiole attaches.

Tiny insignificant white flowers, to one-sixth inch across, form loose open clusters on flower stalks that arise from leaf axils. Tiny fan-shaped petals are smaller than, but similar to, the sepals. Male and female flowers occur separately on the same plant.

The female flowers develop into round black fruits perhaps one-third inch in diameter. The fruits are sometimes mistaken for wild grapes. But the resemblance is only visual. Moonseed fruits are bitter and may have poisonous qualities. In fact, this probably accounts for the infrequent poisonings attributed to wild grapes.

Moonseed fruits contain a single flattened seed that is distinctly crescent or moon-shaped. The ovary in which the seed forms is essentially straight until after fertilization, becoming curved as the fruit matures. The seed is rough, ridged, and so sharp it may cause physical damage to the digestive tract if swallowed. Birds, however, eat the fruits with no apparent damage.

Early Indians had various descriptive names for the inedible fruits such as "sore mouth," "ghost fruit," "thunder grapes," and "grapes of the ghosts." But they sometimes used the root of moonseed plants to treat scrofula.

In pioneer folk medicine, moonseed served as a medical substitute for sarsaparilla. They gave it as a drink to treat weakness resulting from illness and generally as a tonic to improve any condition. A tea of fresh moonseed roots was regarded as a treatment for many human disorders – especially syphilis, rheumatism, skin infections, scrofula and indigestion.

Pioneers also found it useful as a diuretic for treating strangury in horses.

...photograph by Carl Kurtz

Other common names: moccasin flower.

Cypripedium: an incorrectly Latinized version of ancient Greek words meaning "Venus shoe."

Reginae: from Latin meaning "of the queen."

Orchid family: *Orchidaceae.*

Found only rarely in the state, most often in the northern part, on acid soils of bogs and seasonally wet coniferous woods. This endangered species is now protected by legislation in Minnesota where it is the state flower. Flowers June to July.

A single stout leafy stem, grows to more than 2 feet tall, often in clumps of several stems. Stems are coarse and densely covered with somewhat sticky hairs. The stem is leafy to the top, although leaves are less crowded on the upper part.

Leaves grow to 7 inches long and 4 inches wide. They are generally elliptical but pointed at the tip. They narrow toward the base and wrap around the stem. The leaves are alternate with numerous parallel veins which give a corrugated appearance. In general, the plant is coarser and more hairy than the more common yellow lady slipper. The glandular hairs, on the stem and leaves, yield a fatty acid that may cause a rash similar to poison ivy on some people.

The coarse perennial root system develops many stringy and fibrous rootlets.

Each plant usually bears only one or two flowers with a conspicuous white or pink-tinted lip up to 2 inches long. The lip is an inflated sac with a round opening in the top. Margins of the opening are incurved. This "slipper" is actually a specialized petal which gives off a slight fragrance. Three white sepals are longer and broader than the petals, not twisted as in the yellow lady slipper. The two lateral sepals are united under the lip. The lateral petals are narrow and spreading.

Indians and pioneers have long used the *Cypripediums* as a sedative, tranquilizer, or pain reliever. See yellow lady slipper for details. Mythology tells that Orchis, son of a nymph and a satyr, was unattractive but with unbounded passion. Under the influence of drink during a festival of Bacchus, he attacked a priestess. After the angered group tore him limb from limb, his father prayed that he be put back together. The gods refused, but deemed that, despite being a nuisance during life, he should be a pleasure after death – and changed him into a beautiful flower. The flowers of the orchid family are said to retain his temper and passion – and that to eat their root is to suffer momentary conversion into the satyr condition.

C. reginae Walt became the Minnesota state flower after a bit of confusion. *C. calceolus* L. was first so designated, but *C. acaule* Ait. was generally cited as the state flower. When it was discovered that the designated state flower, *C. calceolus* L. was not common in the state, the legislature changed the official state flower to *C. reginae* Walt.

. . . photograph by John Schwegman

Wild leek: *Allium tricoccum* Ait.

Other common names: ramps.

Allium: from Latin, the ancient name for garlic.

Tricoccum: from Latin meaning "three-seeded" referring to grouping of seeds in units of three.

Lily family: *Liliaceae.*

Found throughout the state, usually in colonies, on rich moist soils of woodlands, especially bottomland areas. Flowers appear in June and July.

Two or three broad leaves resembling lily-of-the-valley come up in April or May from a perennial bulb. The leaves are erect, as much as a foot long and 2 inches wide. They are lance-shaped with parallel veins and smooth margins.

A short fibrous rootstock may connect a number of bulbs. The bulb, actually the succulent bases of the leaves, may be as much as 2 inches long. It is seated on and conceals a small dome-shaped stem. Juice of any part of the plant has the strong onion-like odor characteristic of this genus.

Flowers appear after leaves have wilted, and perhaps disappeared. Whitish or yellowish flowers, about one-quarter inch long, cluster into a loose ball at the top of a leafless stalk that may be 15 inches tall. The fruits resemble shiny buckshot arranged in a small ball-like cluster at the top of the stem.

American Indians and pioneers made extensive use of the wild leek leaves and bulbs for seasoning otherwise bland or tasteless foods. The bulbs also served as an emergency food supply. In some cases, pioneer women pickled the bulbs and considered them a delicacy. Insect stings were treated by rubbing juice of a crushed bulb on the affected area. A tea of the bulb effectively induced vomiting.

The Cherokees gathered wild leek bulbs by cutting or breaking off the little stub under the bulb – actually the stem from which roots come – and replanting it so the plant would continue to grow. This is an excellent example of resource conservation, especially since the stem and roots would have been discarded before use anyway.

Wild leek is disliked by dairymen because it imparts a strong and disagreeable flavor to milk when eaten by cows.

The wild leek is credited by some as being part of the origin of the name Chicago. The Menomini Indian term for wild leek, "pikwute sikakushia", means "the skunk." Their term "shi-kako", from which the name Chicago is said to have originated, means "skunk place." Since wild leeks were once abundant in the swampy areas upon which Chicago was built, the connection was considered obvious. *... photograph by Donald R. Kurz*

Wild yam: *Dioscorea villosa* L.

Other common names: China root, colic root, devil's bones, dioscorea, rheumatism root, wild yam root.

Discorea: in honor of the ancient Greek naturalist, Dioscorides.

Villosa: from Latin meaing generally "with hairs."

Yam family: *Dioscoreaceae.*

Found throughout the state, usually in moist woodlands and thickets where it climbs on other vegetation. Blooms June and July.

This perennial has a slender twining stem that grows to 15 feet long. The leaves are heart-shaped, 2 to 6 inches long and 1 to 4 inches across. Margins are smooth or slightly wavy. Leaf petioles are often longer than the leaf blade. They occur alternate along the stem except that lower leaves may be in whorls of three. The pale grayish green undersides of the thin leaves are often downy.

The horizontal rhizomes, usually less than an inch thick, dry to a hard bony texture which gives rise to the name devil's root. Numerous wiry roots extend from the rhizome.

A similar species, *D. quarternata* (Walt.) J.F. Gmel, is found in the southern part of the state. It blooms earlier, has a more erect stem, and has lower leaves in whorls of four or more.

Male and female flowers occur separately. The tiny male flowers, about one tenth of an inch across, are greenish yellow. They occur in drooping clusters of spikelets perhaps 6 inches long.

Female flowers are larger, about one-quarter inch across. These occur on drooping single spikes.

Both the male clusters and the female spikes are on slender stalks attached across the stem from leaf petioles. Close examination shows flower parts occurring in sixes.

The fruits are membraneous triangular capsules about one inch long. Each of three compartments contain one or two seeds. The fruits more conspicuous than the flowers, are sometimes used in dried flower arrangements.

Indians made a tea of the root to relieve pains of child birth and to cure nausea of pregnant women. Dried powdered root was boiled in-water to make a treatment for indigestion.

Pioneers used wild yam for many sorts of intestinal disorders. Southern slaves favored it as a treatment for muscular rheumatism.

Other medicinal uses included treatment for bilious colic, other liver troubles, croup and to induce vomiting.

The tropical food yams belong to this same family.So does the imported Chinese yam or cinnamon vine which has been cultivated as an ornamental and is commonly found as an escape in areas mostly to the east. The edible tubers of one tropical yam, *D. alata* L., may reach a length of 6 to 8 feet and weigh as much as 100 pounds.

. . . photograph by Donald R. Kurz

American bellflower: *Campanula americana,* L.

Other common names: bluebell, tall bellflower.

Campanula: from Latin *campana* for "little bell" referring to the bell-like flowers of some species.

Americana: meaning "of America" since the first identification was made in this country.

Bluebell family: *Campanulaceae.*

Found throughout the state, especially on wet soils of cool shady woodlands and streambanks. Blooms June to frost.

This plant has a slender, straight stem – sometimes with many branches. It grows mostly 3 to 6 feet tall. Alternate leaves 3 to 6 inches long are lance-shaped with pointed tips. They may have a short petiole or no petiole at all. The thin hairy leaves have finely toothed margins. This species is one of the few annuals of the genus.

From a distance, the size, foliage, growth habit and color of the flowers of this species have a strong resemblance to the blue lobelia, *Lobelia syphilitica* L. A closer view shows rather striking differences, however.

The unusual flowers are not truly bell shaped. Five deeply-cut lobes join at the base. The resulting appearance is more as a five-pointed star measuring perhaps an inch across. The delicate blue of the flower shades abruptly to a pale ring at the throat from which emerges a long style (slender tube extending from the ovary). This style curves gently downward with a pronounced up-turn at the tip. Flower buds may bloom at random along the spike-like flower stem. Solitary flowers may also be borne in the axils of upper leaves.

The fruit is a dry capsule which opens at its summit to release the seeds.

A tea brewed from American bellflower leaves was sometimes used in early medicine as a treatment for persistent coughing. The Meskwaki tribe also used such a tea to treat an ailment early writers referred to as consumption – probably tuberculosis and similar problems.

This species was, and sometimes still is, used in gardens for the unusual beauty of the individual flowers. In moist and fertile garden soils, it self-seeds profusely.

A member of the same genus, *C. rapunculoides* L., is the well known rampion of Europe whose leaves and radish-like tap roots are used in salads. This species is sometimes found in the state as an escape from vegetable gardens of pioneer times. Other imported *Campanula* species are grown in flower gardens. Best known is probably *C. medium,* commonly called Canterbury bells. Some additional native species may also be found in the state's woodlands. The other *Campanula* species listed in this book is *C. rotundifolia* L., commonly called harebell – see page 177. *. . . photograph by John Schwegman*

Ginseng: *Panax quinquefolium* L.

Other common names: five-finger.

Panax: from Greek meaning "all remedy" referring to the ancient Chinese belief that the plant was a panacea.

Quinquefolium: from Latin meaning "five-leafed", referring to the five compound parts or leaflets of the three leaves. This species is sometimes listed as *quinquefolius*.

Ginseng family: *Araliaceae*.

Found on humus-rich moist but well drained soils shaded by native hardwoods, never conifers. Once widespread throughout the eastern part of the state, but now increasingly rare. Blooms July to August.

The fleshy perennial rootstock sends up a solitary stem, to 15 inches tall, topped with a single whorl of three compound leaves. Some older plants may have four compound leaves. Each leaf is divided into five leaflets. On occasion, leaflets may number six or even seven. These leaflets are in two sets, two smaller ones at the base and the three larger ones nearer the tip. Margins are finely toothed. Each leaf and leaflet has its own distinct petiole. The roots are relatively large, often forked, and distinctly aromatic.

Ginseng flowers form a pale yellow-green globular mass or cluster on a short stalk arising from the point where leaves branch from the main stem. The leaves form a sort of umbrella above the flower cluster. Individual fowers are tiny, less than an eighth of an inch across, and vary from few to more than 50 in the cluster. The delicate fragrance of the flowers resembles that of lily-of-the-valley.

The fruit is a showy cluster of ruby red berries (shown in photograph), each perhaps a quarter inch in diameter and containing two or three seeds. The cluster of fruits is much more conspicuous and attractive than the flowers.

Roots have been harvested so widely that the plant is now rare. The roots, especially those branched like the two legs of a man, are valued by the Chinese as a remedial agent for fatigue, old age, and sexual impotency. The plant requires about 7 years to develop roots to optimum potential for harvest.

The ginseng name comes from the Chinese "jin-chen", meaning "man-like". Some American Indians called the plant "garantoquen", a word with similar meaning.

Apparently, the effects are more imagined than real, but the commercial value of properly prepared roots remains high enough to cause excessive harvest of the wild ginseng and to encourage cultivation in man-made environments.

Meskwaki and Potawatomi tribes also used ginseng as a love medicine called "a bagger." This mixture of ground ginseng root, mica, gelatin, and snake meat was once regarded as the sure way for a maiden to encourage attentions from a chosen brave.

Early settlers used ginseng for stomach trouble, sore gums, and diarrhea. To be able to eat anything one wanted during a convalescence, a seasoning of ginseng root was added to the desired food.

. . . photograph by Kenneth Formanek

Cow parsnip: *Heracleum lanatum* Michx.

Other common names: masterwort.

Heracleum: from Greek indicating a kind of plant like Hercules, perhaps for its size and strength. Legend also tells that Hercules used this plant in medicine. Or perhaps because Pliny the Elder considered this genus of the highest medical importance.

Lanatum: from Latin for "woolly."

Parsley family: *Apiaceae (Umbelliferae).*

Found throughout the state on low rich soil of moist to wet areas, especially in shady bottomlands. Blooms June through August.

This leafy plant grows to 10 feet tall with a massive stem perhaps 2 inches thick at its base. Despite being hollow, the stem provides sturdy support for this huge plant. The stem is ridged and covered with long white hairs which give a woolly appearance.

Large leaves, to more than a foot across, divide into three segments. Each segment is deeply cut somewhat resembling a maple leaf, whitened with woolly hairs underneath. The long petioles have an inflated sheath where they attach to stem. This sheath and the rank odor are striking characteristics of this plant.

The flowers grow in large flat-topped clusters 8 inches or more across. The clusters are made up of eight to 30 smaller groups. Individual flowers are perhaps a half inch across. They are white, sometimes tinged with pink or purple. Outer petals are larger and unevenly heart-shaped with a shallow notch at the outer end.

The fruits are a flattened broad oval about a half inch long. They are finely hairy and slightly notched at the top.

Despite the disagreeable odor, the cow parsnip is an edible plant. Indians liked the young stems and leaf petioles, both raw and cooked, as a celery-like vegetable. They also boiled the fleshy branched tap root as a potato substitute. Leaves were sometimes used as greens. All this was done with considerable care since it is easy for the novice to mistake the poisonous water hemlock for cow parsnips. Both grow in the same general habitat.

Medical uses for this plant were numerous. Chippewa and Menomini tribes treated fevers and diseases of women with it. Ojibwa and Chippewa tribes powdered and boiled the root to make a poultice for boils.

Dried powdered root was applied to gums for toothache, mixed with fats for rubbing on areas affected with rheumatism, or taken internaly for colic, gas, diarrhea, indigestion, and asthma. Seeds were used for headache. Smoke from burning cow parsnip made an inhalant to revive one who had fainted.

Cow parsnip is sometimes used as an ornamental because of its heavy bold effect.

In parts of the nation bears are sometimes seen feeding on the succulent stems of cow parsnip. *...photograph by Roger Landers*

Wild rose: *Rosa* many species

Other common names: meadow rose, sweet briar.

Rosa: from ancient Latin, the name for "rose."

Species: The wild rose was named state flower of Iowa by the legislature in 1897. Supposedly, any of the native species were therefore the state flower. *Rosa blanda* Ait. (meadow rose) is most often given the honor even though it is common only in the northern half of the state. Easy natural hybridizing makes species difficult to identify.

Rose family: *Rosaceae*.

Found throughout the state under a wide range of conditions, especially in prairies and meadows. It is included here because it is often seen in open woodlands. Blooms June through late summer.

The state's wild roses grow mostly as shrubs to 4 feet tall. Older stems are branched, but newer canes have few branches. Thorns are present in varying numbers. The spreading perennial root system often sends up new shoots.

Leaves usually have five to seven leaflets along a common petiole. They are arranged in opposite pairs except for one at the tip. Leaflets are sharply toothed ovals usually less than 1½ inches long.

Large showy flowers to 2 inches across have five broad petals sometimes with a shallow notch at the outer edge. Solitary or in clusters of a few, they usually appear on new growth branching from older stems. The petals in varying shades of pink are set off by numerous yellow stamens in the center. Five green sepals join to form an urn-shaped base for the bud and flower.

This matures into a smooth red apple-like fruit about a half-inch in diameter. These fruits, or hips, retain their color well into winter.

Meskwaki and Menomini Indians boiled the hips to make a syrup for various food uses. Skins of the hips were used for stomach trouble. Chippewas scraped the second layer of root bark into a cloth, soaked it in water, and squeezed drops of liquid into sore eyes. This was followed immediately by a similar preparation from red raspberry root. Mescalero Apaches boiled rosebuds and drank the resulting liquid as a treatment for gonorrhea.

Both Indians and pioneers ate the hips, flowers, leaves, and new shoots – mostly when other food was scarce. The hips are still an important food for wild life.

Three rose hips (size unspecified) are said to contain as much vitamin C as an orange, and are often sold in natural food stores.

The rose has been cultivated as a garden plant for at least 2000 years. Ancient Greeks, and later Romans, used them in garlands and for social affairs.   *...photograph by LeRoy G. Pratt*

Fringed loosestrife: *Lysimachia ciliata* L.

Other common names: none known.

Lysimachia: probably in honor of the ancient Greek king Lysimachus. Or perhaps from two Greek words *lysis* meaning "a release from" and *mache* meaning "fighting or strife."

Ciliata: from Latin meaning "small hairs", probably in reference to the hairs on the leaf petioles.

Primrose family: *Primulaceae*.

Found throughout the state in moist to wet thickets, woodlands, and streambanks. Blooms June to August.

The smooth slender stem grows erect to 4 feet high. It often divides into several branches.

The leaves are slender pointed ovals as much as 6 inches long and half as wide. Their petioles, perhaps a half inch long, are winged with white curly hairs, from which the descriptive term "fringed" originates. Leaves are opposite along stem except for clusters of small leaves which often occur at the axils of normally-sized leaves.

The perennial rootstock is a slender rhizome.

The flowers, usually less than an inch across, have five pure yellow petals with a reddish tinge at their base which forms a ring in the center of the flower. The distinctive petals are almost circular, but with a sharp point at the tip. The outer edge on either side of the point is sometimes ragged, giving the appearance of having been gnawed lightly by a rodent. Each flower is carried nodding or erect on its own slender stalk which arises from a leaf axil. Flower stalks may be as long as 2 inches.

Despite the beauty of individual flowers, the plant is rather inconspicuous because the foliage so dominates the scattered flowers.

The fruit is a five-celled capsule usually less than three-fourths inch long. Each cell contains several small seeds.

Authorities differ on the genera to which the loosestrifes belong. Some would list as *Lysimacha* those species with stamens joined at their base to a sleeve-like ring fitted around the central ovary. Species without stamens joined at their base would be placed in the genus *Steironema*. Other authorities feel that the two types belong in the same genera.

No medicinal or food uses of fringed loosestrife are known.

Legends tell that King Lysimachus of Thrace (an ancient kingdom now divided between Greece and Turkey) was being chased by an angry bull. To escape he grabbed a plant of loosestrife and waved it before the bull which quickly quieted down. As a result, the plant was long considered to pacify angry people as well as animals. Any real effect must have been mostly psychological.

Several other species of loosestrife are found in the state. The common garden loosestrife *(L. vulgaris* L.) is a European species that has escaped to the wild in much of our area. This species is sometimes used by herbalists in conjunction with other herbs to brew a tea for controlling bleeding – hemorrhage, nosebleed, excess menstrual flow, and even wounds.

. . . photography by Kitty Kohout

Other common names: beggarlice, burrhead, cleavers, flea-weed, goosegrass, gripgrass, itchweed, loveman, love-me plant, pigtails, poor robin, scrachweed, sweethearts.

Galium: from Greek for "milk", referring to use of some species to curdle milk for cheesemaking.

Species: Four of the more common species in the state are: *G. aparine* L. is an annual blooming in May and June. *G. concinnum* Torr. and Gray is a perennial that blooms in June and July. *G. triflorum* Michx. is a perennial with a June-August blooming period. *G. tinctorium* L.is a perennial that blooms May to July.

Madder family: *Rubiaceae.*

Found throughout the state, especially on moist rich sandy or alluvial soils of low woodlands and prairies. Various species bloom May to August.

The fine stems of this genus are often weak and sprawling, especially in the annual species. Most are four-angled. Some species have distinct bristles and hairy joints. The slender stems may be profusely branched, sometimes erect and woody at the base. Height may vary from a few inches to 4 feet or more. Small leaves occur in whorls – usually of four, sometimes of six or eight. Leaves are usually slender, pointed at each end, and rough at both margins and mid-ribs.

Sparse and modest flowers are white in most species, sometimes greenish or yellow. They are borne in loose clusters, usually of three flowers or less, upon stalks arising from axils of upper leaves. Tiny flowers are usually saucer-shaped and about an eighth of an inch across. In most species, flowers have four petals, but some have only three petals which are joined at the base. The inconspicuous flowers draw little notice, but bristles of the fruits and plant parts tend to stick to clothing and become quite a conspicuous nuisance.

As the name bedstraw implies, it was once used as a filler for home-made mattresses. Because branches tended to stick together, the thickness remained relatively uniform even after periods of use. One species with yellow flowers has a pleasant fragrance and was particularly desired for mattresses.

Legend tells that the manger where the Christ Child was born contained bedstraw *(G. verum* L.). Folklore also has it that if a newly married couple filled their mattress with bedstraw, they would be blessed with many children.

Young bedstraw plants have been used as greens. Seeds have served as a coffee substitute – the coffee plant is a member of this family. The leaves have been used to curdle milk for making cheese.

Roots some species, especially *G. tinctorium* L., have been used as a source of red-purple dye.

Medicinal properties once attributed to bedstraw include easing childbirth, slowing the flow of blood, increasing urine flow, stimulating the appetite, reducing fever, correcting vitamin C deficiency, treating skin rashes, and soothing nerves.

It has even been used as a wash intended to remove freckles.

. . . photograph by LeRoy G. Pratt

Wild petunia: *Ruellia humilis* Nutt.

Other common names: hairy ruellia.

Ruellia: in honor of an early French herbalist, Jean de la Ruelle (1474-1537).

Humilis: from Latin meaning "low" in obvious reference to the ground-hugging appearance of this species in many environments. The *Ruellia* genus is so variable that some authorities combine this species with another called *Ruellia caroliniensis* (Walt.) Stend.

Acanthus family: *Acanthaceae.*

Found throughout the state in open woodlands, especially where soils are rocky or sandy and in prairies. Blooms June through August.

The stout and much branched stem of this species grows mostly a few inches tall, but may range on up to 3 feet. The stems are usually hairy and several arise from a common fibrous perennial root system. Internodes of the stem are short – usually shorter than the leaves. In general, the appearance is short, bushy, and leafy. In some cases it is so low-growing that it appars to be a creeping groundcover type of plant.

The four to 12 pairs of leaves are pointed ovals seldom more than 3 inches long. Most leaves are about the same size except that both those at the top and at the bottom maybe slightly smaller.

Margins of the leaves are without teeth. The whole leaf has a leathery texture and may be hairy, especially along the veins and margins. The leaves are usually without petioles – or sometimes with very short petioles.

The showy petunia-like flowers are light lavender to purple, rarely white. They are smaller and less flared than the common petunia (which belongs in another plant family, *Solomanaceae*). The outer part of the flare is indented to give five shallow lobes. The flowers are borne singly or clustered, usually without individual flower stalks, in the axils of all but the lower leaves.

The lobes, or petals, join to form a tubular base. The total blossom may be as much as 3 inches long including a tube as much as 2 inches long. Most are smaller than this, however. In addition to these showy flowers, a few may remain unopened and bud-like – and are self-fertilized. The term for this sort of flower is "cleistogamous."

The fruit is a dry oval capsule usually less than three-fourths inch long. It contains several small roundish seeds. The calyx surrounding the capsule has five slender segments which are quite hairy and which extend beyond the fruit capsule.

The *Ruellia* species are extremely variable over much of their range.

No food or medicinal uses by Indians or pioneers are known.

While most of the *Acanthus* family are confined to tropical areas of the western hemisphere, leaves of a Mediterranean *Acanthus* are said to have been the inspiration for the design at the top of ancient Greek Corinthian columns.

. . . photograph by Donald R. Kurz

Catnip: *Nepeta cataria* L.

Other common names: catmint, catnep, catrup, catwort, field balm, nip.

Nepeta: from Latin – an old name for several of the mints, thought to be derived from Nepeta, an ancient Etruscan city.

Cataria: from Latin meaning "has to do with cats."

Mint family: *Lamiaceae (Labiatae).*

Found throughout the state in open woods, especially woodland edges. Blooms June to September.

Leafy stems grow erect with many branches and may be as tall as 3 feet. The stem is downy and squarish, four-angled, typical of the mint family. An extensive perennial root system makes this plant an aggressive competitor.

Leaves are opposite and on long petioles. They are a dark grey-green above, lighter beneath because of numerous soft whitish hairs. Leaves tend to be less numerous near the top of the plant. They are mostly 2 to 3 inches long, shaped as long ovals pointed at the tip, or as arrowheads. Margins have coarse teeth which may appear as notches or scallops.

The foliage is dotted with small glands containing a volatile oil responsible for the minty, but not unpleasant, odor when a leaf is crushed. This may also account for the fact that catnip is free from insect and fungus pests, an unusual feature.

Flowers, mostly one-fourth to one half inch long, are borne in relatively small coarse clusters. These dense spike-like clusters may be as much as 4 inches long. The individual two-lipped flowers are white to pale blue. The lower lip is wider, dotted with purple and has three lobes. The upper lip is slightly hooded and has a shallow notch rather than pronounced lobes. The fruits are small brown oval nutlets with paired white spots at one end.

Mohican Indians used a catnip tea and considered it especially good for infants with colic. Other tribes, including the Ojibwas, used the leaves as a tea substitute.

Both early settlers and Indians considered catnip tea useful for increasing menstrual flow. Other pioneer uses were extensive – stomach disorders, fever, infant colic, respiratory problems, hives, and nervous disorders. It also rated high as a general tonic and as a beverage. The leaves served as a poultice to reduce swellings. Fresh leaves have been used to flavor sauces and cooked foods; dried leaves in herb mixtures for soups and stews. All cats, including lions and tigers, are attracted to catnip. In fact, it is often considered a feline aphrodisiac. It is used in toys for cats.

Trappers often bait their traps with oil extracted from catnip for attracting bobcats and mountain lions.

There was once a run on catnip toys by drug addicts who suspected that if it gave cats a "high", it might do the same for them.

Catnip is an alien, naturalized from Europe, probably as plantings in early herb gardens.   ...*photograph by William Welker*

Ground cherry: *Physalis heterophylla* Nees.

Other common names: clammy ground cherry, husk tomato.

Physalis: from Greek meaning "bladder", in reference to the bladder-like seed husk.

Heterophylla: from Greek *hetero* for "varied" and from *phylla* for "leaves", describing the wide variety of leaf shapes found in this species. Several other species with similar flowers and fruits are also found in the state. The common Chinese lantern plant, *P. franchetti* Mast. is one of them.

Nightshade family: *Solanaceae.*

Found throughout the state on rich, well drained soils of woodlands, fence rows, and open areas. Flowers June to September.

This plant may grow to 3 feet tall as either a single or a much branched stem. Since the stem tends to be weak, it may be partially reclining with only the tips fully erect. The stem is hairy, and its hairs secrete a substance which makes the stem feel slightly sticky. The deep perennial underground root system often has many branches.

The alternate leaves are broadly oval, usually 2 to 4 inches long, and quite varied in shape. Margins may have shallow blunt teeth and be either lobed or wavy. The leaf base tends to be more rounded than in other *Physalis* species. Prominent veins join inside leaf margins.

Nodding, bell-like flowers, to an inch across, are borne singly on short stalks arising from leaf axils. The "bell" is somewhat fluted or pleated with five shallow lobes. The flower is a modest greenish-yellow with a brown or bluish center.

The fruit is a yellow, many-seeded berry about the size of a small cherry. It is enclosed in a crisp, paper-like husk, usually about an inch long. The husk is five-angled and pointed at the tip. The husk tends to protect the fruit for some time after being dropped to the ground. The berries often drop to the ground while still somewhat green, but they finish ripening on the ground. Upon ripening, the flavor is somewhat sweet but generally regarded as rather bland.

Fruits are edible when ripe but should be avoided when green. They have a strong unpleasant flavor and contain a mildly toxic substance until ripe. Livestock have been poisoned by eating large amounts of the green berries and leaves, but only when other feed is short.

Indians and pioneers ate ground cherries either raw or cooked. The cooked form was usually sauce in the case of Indians; pies or preserves in the case of pioneers. The ground cherry is still cutivated in gardens, and fruits are sometimes sold in markets.

Ground cherries were sometimes used as a poultice for snake bite. A tea brewed from the plant was said to cure dropsy. Indians of the Meskwaki tribe thought the tea would cure a spell of dizziness.

Insects, birds and rodents find ground cherry fruits a favorite source of late fall nutrition. *...photograph by Ruth Fagen*

False dragonhead: *Physostegia virginiana* (L.) Benth.

Other common names: dragon head, lion's heart, obedient plant.

Physostegia: from Greek meaning "bladder covering" referring to the somewhat inflated appearance of the flower. An earlier generic name was *Dracocephalum* which in Latin meant literally "dragon head."

Virginiana: referring to where the plant was first found and studied.

Mint family: *Lamiaceae (Labiatae).*

Found throughout the state in moist to wet woodlands, usually along streams and in thickets. Blooms June to September.

The square stem, typical of the mint family, grows erect to 4 feet tall in favorable sites. It may be branched toward the top. The opposite leaves are narrow lance shapes, 2 to 5 inches long and seldom more than one inch wide. Upper leaves are much smaller than lower ones. Lower leaves have short petioles while upper ones have none. Margins of the leaves have many sharp teeth which curve slightly inward at their tips.

The spreading fibrous perennial root system sends up new plants, so false dragonhead often appears in dense colonies.

Flowers are borne in a terminal spike 4 to 8 inches long. Individual flowers, each about an inch long, cluster close together in vertical rows along the spike. They are mostly pale purple to rose colored.

Shape of the flower resembles the snapdragon, resulting in the common name false dragonhead. It is a little more funnel-shaped, with an open gaping mouth.

The upper lip is arching and hood-like. The lower lip is three-lobed. The middle lobe itself has additional shallow notches. The lower lip tends to be lighter colored, often spotted with darker purple.

The flowers grow in vertical rows along the spike. If flowers of a row are pushed to the right or left of their row, they tend to remain in that position for considerable time. This unusual characteristic gives rise to the common name, obedient plant.

The fruiting calyx which encloses the four-celled ovary is usually less than one half inch long. It remains open at the tip with its five lobes flaring outward slightly. The smooth brown nutlets inside are three-sided ovals with the surfaces somewhat channeled.

Because of its beauty, this native flower has been and is still used in flower gardens. Other uses by Indians or pioneers are not known. But for treating common colds, the Meskwaki tribe made a tea of the leaves from a closely related species also found in the state, *P. parviflora* Nutt.

. . . photograph by Marlin Bowles

Fireweed: *Epilobium angustifolium* L.

Other common names: blooming Sally, blooming willow, fire-top, French willow herb, great willow herb, Persian willow, purple rocket, wickup, wicopy.

Epilobium: from Greek meaning "upon or above the pod", referring to the manner in which the flowers keep blooming above the seed pods maturing lower on the flower spike.

Angustifolium: from Latin for "narrow leaf."

Evening primrose family: *Onagraceae.*

Found through the northern part of the state. It most often occurs as one of the early species in burned-over areas, or where soil has been recently disturbed. Also at woodland edges, often growing in patches. Blooms June to September.

Strong erect stems grow to 7 feet tall from a perennial crown. They may be lightly branched or unbranched, smooth or somewhat downy. Alternate lance-shaped leaves, to 6 inches long and an inch wide, are dark green above but lighter underneath. They have short petioles, smooth margins, and veins which curve to meet the adjoining vein rather than extending to the leaf margin.

Purple to pink, rarely white, flowers are quite showy. Individual flowers, perhaps a inch across, have four rounded petals each about a half inch long. Flowers may appear over the entire season on a single plant. Blooming begins at the bottom of the tightly clustered flower spike and progresses upward. A single flower spike will have the typically drooping buds at the top with colorful flowers in the middle and long erect reddish seed pods toward the bottom, all at the same time. Fireweed flowers are a favorite source of nectar for honeybees.

When ripe, pods burst open to release numerous tiny seeds, each with a tuft of fluffy hairs so it can easily float along with the wind.

The roots were used to wash swellings, as a poultice for boils, and as a rectal injection for hermorrhoids. Chippewas used fresh leaves, or dried leaves made moist, as poultice for bruises or splinters.

Western Indians scooped the pith from large stalks to eat raw, cook as a thick soup, or bake into bread. The leaves have been used to make tea. New shoots have been eaten raw or cooked like asparagus. French Canadians call the plant "asperge" or wild asparagus.

A horticultural variety of this species was developed in England for planting in flower gardens. It grows as a compact bush with white flowers which are suitable for cutting.

Among other species of *Epilobium* found in the state are *E. coloratum* Bichler, *E. adenocaulon* Haussk., *E. strictum* Muhl., and *E. leptophyllum* Raf. These species are commonly called willow herbs and generally inhabit boggy areas. All somewhat resemble the fireweed.   *...photograph by James P. Rowan*

Harebell: *Campanula rotundifolia* L.

Other common names: blue bells of Scotland, fairy bells, fairy thimbles, heath bells, ladies' thimbles, Scottish bluebells, thimbles, witches' bells.

Campanula: from Latin *campana* in the diminutive form meaning "little bell" and referring to the shape or the flower.

Rotundifolia: from Latin meaning "round leaf" in reference to the shape of the early basal leaves. A related species, *C. aparinoides* Pursh., is also known in the state.

Bluebell family: *Campanulaceae.*

Found sparingly in about the northern half of the state on gravel or sandy soils of dry or well drained woods, slopes, and meadows. *C. aparinoides* Pursh. is found, now rarely, on wet streambanks and in meadows of the same area. Blooms June to September.

The thin wiry stems of this slender delicate perennial grow to 18 inches tall from rosettes of basal leaves. The stem may be sparsely branched or unbranched. The irregularly circular leaves of the basal rosette are small, to an inch across. They have toothed margins and are on long petioles. There is a deep cleft where the petiole attaches to the leaf blade. These leaves wither early and are seldom still present at time of flowering.

Numerous leaves alternate along the stem are unlike the basal leaves – linear, almost hair-like, and without teeth on the margins. They are usually one to 3 inches long and tend to angle upward from the point where they attach to the stem.

The perennial root system is relatively small, consisting of fibrous rootlets and sprawling white rhizomes. The rhizomes are brittle and easily broken.

C. aparinoidies Pursh. is somewhat similar in vegetative apperance. But its stems are rough and clinging, more like bedstraw. It is known locally both as marsh bellflower and as bedstraw bellflower.

The beautiful violet bells, three-fourths to an inch long, nod from the tips of the plant's sparse branches. The flared edge of the flower bell has five broad lobes with pointed tips. Buds, flowers, and seeds are commonly found on a stem at the same time. Often, a solitary bloom may be found after other plants have stopped growing for the season.

Flowers of *C. aparinoides* Pursh. are smaller and are white to pale blue.

Fruits of both are short oval capsules containing several tiny smooth seeds.

The Campanula genus, native to the whole northern hemisphere, includes species cultivated in flower gardens and the rampion of European salads. The edible white rampion tubers are grown especially for this purpose.

No medical or food uses of this plant by Indians or pioneers are known. Cheyenne Indians, however, used this species in some of their religious ceremonies. Wild animals commonly feed upon the sparse harebell foliage.

. . . photograph by Kenneth Frazier

Other common names: convulsion weed, corpse plant, Dutchman's pipe, fairy smoke, ghost flower, ice plant, pipe plant.

Monotropa: from Greek menaing "one turn", referring to the sharp recurving of top of the stem.

Uniflora: from Latin meaning "one flower."

Wintergreen family: *Pyrolaceae (Ericaceae).*

Found throughout the state in shady woods on moist humus-rich soils. Stems may be solitary, but most often occur in clumps. Appears June to September.

The fleshy stem, clammy to the touch, grows to one foot tall. Its color is a waxy pinkish white when fresh, maturing to black before becoming dry and brown. Even touching the plant can cause it to blacken. The stems, usually several, arise from a mat of brittle fibrous roots which obtain nutrients from decaying organic material. Botanists disagree on whether or not the roots obtain the nutrients directly or indirectly through fungi in the organic material.

The only leaves are rudimentary, appearing scale-like alternately along the stem. The plant has no chlorophyl (green coloring matter) with which to manufacture its own food from soil nutrients, carbon dioxide, sunlight and water.

Solitary odorless flowers are borne at the tops of the stems, first drooping to form the "pipe", then becoming erect as the fruit forms. The flowers, to one inch long, have four to six whitish petals which tend to flare at the outer end into a shape that faintly resembles that of a bell or of the bowl of a smoker's pipe.

The fruit is a vase-shaped five-celled seed capsule about two-thirds of an inch long and half as wide. Each cell contains many small seeds.

Widest medical use of Indian pipe has been for treating sore eyes. Both Indian tribes and early settlers considered it useful for this purpose. Clear juice from the stem – sometimes diluted with water – was dropped directly into the eye. Early pioneer doctors sometimes used the dried plant as a sedative, to ease pain, to reduce nervousness, and to treat epilepsy and other convulsions.

Although Indian pipe is in a family which includes some poisonous plants, there are at least two reports of the plant having been cooked and eaten as food.

One Indian legend tells that this plant always appeared on the exact spot where some Indian had knocked the white ashes of his pipe on the forest floor.

Another species with scented multiple flowers, *M. hypopithys* L., is found less frequently. It is best known by the common name pinesap.   *...photograph by LeRoy G. Pratt*

Lopseed: *Phryma leptostachya* L.

Other common names: none known.

Phryma: origin of this generic name is lost in antiquity. This is the only genus known in its family.

Leptostachya: from Latin meaning "slender-spiked", a logical description for the flower spike. Recent reports indicate that two additional species may have been found in Asia.

Lopseed family: *Phrymaceae.*

Found throughout the state on fertile soils of moist shady woods. Flowers June through September.

This unusual plant grows to 3 feet tall. It's stem is four-angled as with the mint family. But it is dark green, unlike the mints. It grows erect and is generally branched toward the top. It may be smooth or slightly hairy. Joints show distinct enlargement.

The thin bright green leaves are opposite along the stem. Those on the lower part of the stem have long petioles. Upper leaves have short petioles or none at all. Leaf size varies from 2 to 4 inches long. They are generally oval in shape, broader at the base and tapering to a sharp tip. Pronounced marginal teeth are shallow but prolonged and often double. The veins join inside the margins.

Tiny purplish snapdragon-like flowes are seldom much more than a quarter inch long. Close examination reveals two distinct lips. The upper is erect and notched. The lower is much longer and divided into three spreading bluntly rounded lobes. The flowers are borne in opposite pairs, each at right angles to the stem. Pairs are well separated along the 3 to 6 inch flower stalks. A portion of the flower stalk is bare between the upper leaves and the flower spike.

Buds are erect, extending upward along the stem. Flowers are at right angles to the stem when in full bloom. As the flowers mature, they "lop" down against the stem, giving rise to the common name of "lopseed".

The fully ripe seeds seem to hide an inner spring. When touched, they may break free and snap outward, often to a distance of a foot or more. Each seed has three slender hooked teeth at one end by which they attach weakly to clothing or to animals.

No food or medicinal uses by Indians or early pioneers are known. The plant is sometimes grown in gardens – for its botanical interest rather than its beauty.

. . . photograph by Roger Landers

Milkwort: *Polygala sanguinea* L.

Other common names: candyroot, field milkwort, pink milkwort, purple milkwort, rattlesnake root, seneca snakeroot, strawberry tassel.

Polygala: from Greek meaning "much milk", probably originating from an ancient belief that certain plant species, if eaten by cattle, would increase the flow of milk.

Sanguinea: from Latin for "blood red", referring to the color of the tiny flowers. A closely related species, *P. senega* (Tourn.) L., derived its name from the Seneca Indian tribe.

Milkwort family: *Polygalaceae.*

Found throughout the state on rich, well drained soils. Some species prefer rocky or sandy soils. Some prefer light shade while others favor open areas and meadows. Blooms June through September.

Species of our area range from 2 to 20 inches tall. Various species are annual, biennial, or perennial. Stems are mostly erect, slender but tough. Some may be sparsely branched toward the top. Leaves are mostly alternate, lance shaped, and without petioles. A few species have leaves in whorls. The annual *P. sanguinea* L. (shown) grows to 15 inches tall with alternate leaves evenly distributed along the stem. These leaves are linear, as much as one and one-fourth inch long and one-sixth of an inch wide. The perennial *P. senega* (Tourn.) L. is slightly larger and has its leaves more evenly distributed on the upper part of the stem.

Many species have flowers of striking beauty. *P. sanguinea* L. has tiny rose-purple sometimes greenish-white, flowers clustered in a flat-topped spike about three-fourths inch across. *P. senega* (Tourn.) L., the Seneca snakeroot, has dense spikes of small white flowers. After the flowers fall, small bracts remain on the flower spike so that it keeps its distinctive shape.

Examination under magnification shows five sepals. The upper most and two lower ones are small and often greenish. The two lateral sepals, larger and colored like petals, are called "wings." Three petals and the stamen tube are joined together. The middle lower petal is keel-shaped and generally fringed. These parts are often partially concealed by the more prominent wings. The seeds are borne one per cavity (one per flower) in the head. They are generally oval in shape and quite hairy.

Some species also form underground flowers that do not open but develop fruits – much as hog peanuts do.

Meskwaki and Potawatomi tribes boiled the root and used it as a drink to treat heart trouble.

Pioneers used *Polygala* species as an expectorant for acute bronchitis, spasmodic croup, and catarrhal laryngitis.

Early pioneers took a special but temporary interest in *P. senega* (Tourn.) L. after learning that Seneca Indians chewed the root and applied it to snake bites – perhaps because the twisted root reminded them of a snake. Ottawa and Chippewa tribes boiled the bark and used the resulting tea in attempts to induce abortion.

...photograph by Bruce Plum

Monkey flower: *Mimulus ringens* L.

Other common names: square-stemmed monkey flower

Mimulus: from Latin meaning generally "mimic" or "monkey" in diminutive form, referring to the unusual monkey-face shape of the flower.

Ringens: from Latin meaning "gaping," also referring to the flower, especially its open-mouthed appearance.

Snapdragon family: *Scrophulariaceae.*

Found throughout the state, but rare in the southern parts. It prefers partial shade of wet places, especially swamps and along stream banks. Flowers June to September

The squarish or four-angled stem grows erect, mostly one to 3 feet tall. It is smooth and has numerous branches. The narrow lance-shaped leaves are 2 to 4 inches long and about a half-inch across. They are rounded at the base and pointed toward the outer end. Conspicuous veins join inside the coarsely toothed margins. Leaves are opposite and without petioles, some clasping the stem.

The perennial root system is fibrous and extensive, often forming dense mats of stolons and slender rhizomes.

With sufficient imagination, one can see the grinning face of a tiny monkey in the showy violet-purple flower. Squeeze the sides of the flower to widen the "grin" and increase the resemblance to a monkey face. Rarely, the flower color may be pinkish or even white. They appear as single blossoms on long slender flower stalks arising from the axils of upper leaves. Since the leaves are opposite, the flowers are also paired along the tops of the stem branches.

The tubular flowers, about an inch along, flare into two lips resembling those of the snapdragon. The upper lip is two-lobed and erect. The lower lip is three-lobed and spreading. A prominent yellow two-ridged palate nearly closes the throat of the flower. The long green five-angled calyx base from which the flower emerges has five sharp uneven teeth.

The dry fruit capsule has two lobes, each containing many tiny seeds.

Young leaves and stems were used as salad greens by western Indians. Early cowboys sometimes made a poultice of monkey flower to treat rope burns.

Some species are cultivated for their unusual and beautiful flowers. They are especially suited to gardens in which soils are wet.

Two other species of Mimulus are found in the state. *M. glabratus* HBK. is yellow flowered and grows, sparsely, around springs and seeps in the northern part of the state. *M. alatus* Ait. has violet purple flowers and a "winged" stem. It is common in the southern half of the state; rare in the northern half.

. . . photograph by W. K. Hollingsworth

Stinging nettle: *Urtica dioica* L.

Other common names: wood nettle.

Urtica: from Latin now meaning "nettle." The original Latin derivation was probably from *uro* meaning "to burn." Another stinging nettle more common in parts of Indiana is similar but of a different genus – *Laportea canadensis* (L.) Wedd.

Dioica: from Greek meaning "two households", referring to the fact that male and female flower parts are borne separately.

Nettle family: *Urticaceae.*

Found throughout the state on rich moist soils in open areas or light shade. Flowers June to September.

An erect unbranched stem, covered with short bristly hairs, grows to 8 feet tall. It is hollow, fibrous, and squarish in cross section.

Closely spaced leaves are opposite, coarsely toothed, and conspicuously veined. Leaves to 4 inches long are broad at the base and tapered to a pointed tip. Lower leaves may show a pronounced heart shape. Petioles are no longer than half the width of the leaf. Bristly hairs are also found on the leaf blades of this perennial.

Another nettle in the same family, *Laportea canadensis* (L.) Wedd., has generally finer features and alternate leaves.

Tiny green flowers, individually inconspicuous, occur in branched clusters arising from the leaf axils. Most clusters are about half as long as the leaves. Male and female flowers are usually on the same plant.

Each tiny hair on the stem and leaves is hollow with a jagged point at its tip and a bulb at its base. A bump against the stiff hair squeezes the bulb, forcing an irritating chemical (probably formic acid) through the hair, much like the action of a miniature hypodermic needle. The sting can be lessened by rubbing the affected area with the nettle's own root or with juice of jewelweed.

Paralyzed limbs were whipped with the fresh plant to stimulate muscles into action – a process called flagellation or urtication – in the Middle Ages. Later the nettle was used in a similar manner for rheumatism. Seeds of the plant were also used to treat for internal parasites and as a hypnotic drug.

A poultice of leaves soaked in warm water was used for heat rash. Watery juice from cooked nettles was said to cure dandruff and falling hair. A non-alchololic "nettle beer" was considered especially good for old people.

Fibers of the mature plant once served as a substitute for hemp to produce nets and rope. At one time, the fiber was used in Scotland to make nettle linen, considered more beautiful and more durable than linen made from flax.

Young shoots of stinging nettle are still considered excellent for greens. Protein content of the leaves is high – perhaps the reason nettle greens were favored for persons trying to lose weight. Dried nettle foliage also makes a good animal feed.

A yellow dye can be obtained from roots of the plant.

. . . photograph by William Welker

Tick trefoil: *Desmodium* several species

Other common names: beggar's lice, stick tights.

Desmodium: from Greek meaning "long branch or chain", probably from the shape and attachment of the seedpods.

Species: Several species are found in the state. Most common are *D. glutinosum* Muhl., *D. canadense* (L.), *D. dillenii* Darl., and *D. paniculatum* (L.) D.C. Differences among species are mostly technical and of little consequence since fruits of all of the state's species have the same annoying property of clinging tenaciously to clothing.

Legume family: *Fabaceae (Leguminosae).*

Found throughout the state under a wide variety of conditions from dry to wet soils and from open woodlands to prairie, depending upon the species. Flowering is from June through September.

Plants are mostly less than 3 feet tall, though some species may grow to more than twice that under favorable conditions. The stems tend to be spindly, sometimes erect and sometimes trailing. They are generally hairy. Some are unbranched; some are profusely branched.

Leaves are alternate along the stem, but tend to be concentrated toward the top of the plant. Most leaves are divided into three leaflets. The petiole of the main leaf is usually about as long as one of the leaflets. The smooth-margined leaflets are pointed ovals of varying width.

The perennial root systems vary considerably among species, but tend to be deep and extensive. Bacteria living in nodules on the roots take nitrogen from the air and convert it into a form that can be used by the plant. This characteristic, typical of the legume family, is one of nature's ways of slowly improving soil fertility.

Flowers, having the shape typical of peas and other legumes, are showy but small. Their color is usually rosy-purple to magenta-pink, rarely white. They are usually less than a half inch across. Numerous flowers are borne at the tips of the upper branches, but only a few are in bloom at any one time. Seed pods, blooming flowers, and buds may all appear on a single stem at the same time.

Fruits are flattened pods with a triangular segment for each seed. The hairy pods break apart easily at the segments and cling to animals or clothing. Tiny hairs with a hook at the end are the means by which the pod segments attach themselves firmly to clothing or to animals. This is nature's way of distributing seeds to new areas. The pods, seldom as much as one inch long, usually have three to five segments and may be sharply indented between segments.

No uses of this plant, by Indians or pioneers are known, but the sticky fruits assure that these species were as much a nuisance then as they are today.

There has been some experimenting with species of *Desmodium* for possible use as a forage crop in this country and in other areas of the world. *. . . photograph by Ruth Fagen*

Other common names: American nightshade, cancer-jalap, coakum, ganget, inkberry, pacan bush, pigeonberry, pokeweed, red ink plant, redweed, skoke.

Phytolacca: from Greek *phyto* meaning "plant" and probably from medieval Latin *lacca* meaning "crimson-lake", referring to the red juice of the berries.

Americana: indicating first identification made in this country.

Pokeweed family: *Phytolaccaceae.*

Found throughout the state, mostly in groups of a few plants at woodland edges. Also found in the open woods on either wet or dry soils. Blooms June to October.

A hollow, thick but weak stem to 10 feet tall grows from a fleshy perennial root system. The stem and its branches often display a distinct reddish or purplish coloring.

Large dark green leaves grow to 10 inches long on thick petioles. They are shaped as a lance-head, pointed at both ends. Margins are wavy but without teeth. Leaves are alternate along the stem.

Small, seldom more than one-fourth inch across, greenish white flowers are borne in spike-like racemes arising opposite the petioles of upper leaves. What appear to be four or five petals are really sepals.

Fruits are dark purple berries which remain on the plant long after the leaves have been killed by frost. Each berry may be as much as a half inch in diameter and contains five to 15 small seeds.

Iroquois Indians – and perhaps others – were using pokeberry shoots (picked early before they develop the purple coloring) as food when the first explorers arrived on this continent. The plant was then taken to Europe for the same purpose. It was described as a substitute for asparagus.

Indians also used the powdered root as a poultice to treat cancer and fever. Early settlers used juice of the berries to treat skin sores. The root, mixed with lard, made a treatment for many skin disorders. A bit of the root also made a powerful, but dangerous, emetic. It has also been used to relieve itching of the eye.

Pokeberry juice served as dye and as ink. Many a Civil War soldier wrote home using a hand-made turkey quill pen and red pokeberry ink. Some of those letters still exist today.

The common name "poke" is believed to derive from the Indian word "pocan" meaning plant that yields yellow or red dye.

Pokeberry roots and seeds are poisonous. Children have been poisoned by eating the berries – probably more from the seeds rather than flesh of the berries. Birds, however, feed extensively on pokeberries and escape ill effects – perhaps by excreting the seeds.   *...photograph by John Schwegman*

Wild cucumber: *Echinocystis lobata* (Michx.) T. & G.

Other common names: balsam apple, creeping Jennie, squirting cucumber.

Echinocystis: from the Greek *echinos* for "hedgehog" and *kystis* for "bladder" in reference to the prickly fruit.

Lobata: from Latin meaning "lobed" for the lobed leaves.

Gourd family: *Cucurbitaceae.*

Found in the northern three-fourths of the state on rich moist soils, especially along stream banks and woodlands borders. Flowers June to October.

This annual climbing and branching vine, to 25 feet long, has a slender grooved stem that is quite weak. It clings to other plants or fences with coiling tendrils which occur opposite the leaves. Tendrils may be branched into three forks. The presence of a wild cucumber does not seem to harm the supporting plant except perhaps to compete for sunlight. Sometimes hairs occur at or near the joints.

Leaves, to 3 inches long, are on petioles often as long as the leaf. Three to seven pointed lobes give a characteristic shape resembling an irregular star. Leaves are typically wider than they are long. Both upper and lower surfaces may feel somewhat rough to the touch. Margins have small teeth, usually widely spaced.

Tiny greenish-yellow flowers less than a half inch across are either male or female. Male flowers are borne abundantly in loose open clusters that may be as much as 12 inches long.

Female flowers occur singly or in pairs on their own short stalks at the base of the male flower cluster. Stalks of both types of flowers arise from leaf axils. Each flower has six slender spreading petals about one-third inch long. Petals are joined near their base.

Fertilized female flowers become green, egg-shaped fruits about 2 inches long and one inch in diameter. This fruit, spongy and sparsely covered with spines, is not edible. It soon dries out and bursts at the tip. This bursting may expel the four large flat brownish seeds which are rounded at one end and bluntly pointed at the other. Each seed has a hard thick rough covering.

Pioneers sometimes used a root tea for stomach troubles and as a general tonic. A poultice of pulverized root was used for headache.

Some Indian tribes used the root as a general remedy for a wide range of disorders. Among these tribes were the Meskwaki who called the plant "mishinawe" meaning generally man-in-the-ground.

Wild cucumber has been used for landscaping. As one of our woodland's fastest growing vines, it is sometimes used to hide objects while slower growing plants develop.

A somewhat similar plant is the bur cucumber (*Sicyos angulatus* L.). It has more hairs, flowers with five instead of six petals, and smaller fruits borne in clusters.

In the same family with wild cucumber are some common garden plants including cucumber, squash, pumpkins and melons.

. . . photograph by Marlin Bowles

Yarrow: *Achillea lanulosa* Nutt.

Other common names: gordaldo, milfoil, nosebleed weed, old man's pepper, sanguinary, soldier's woundwort.

Achillea: named for the mythological Greek hero Achilles who is said to have used the plant to heal wounds of soldiers after battle.

Lanulosa: from Latin meaning "woolly or downy" referring to the webby hairs covering the plant.

Daisy family: *Asteraceae (Compositae).*

Found widely throughout the state in open woodlands, woods edges, roadsides, and open areas, especially on well drained sandy or gravel type soils. Blooms June to frost.

The slender stiff erect stem to 2 feet tall is seldom branched below the flowerheads. It is usually covered with fine webby hairs which give the plant a woolly appearance. A similar species introduced from Europe, *A. millefolium* L., usually has a less woolly stem and coarser leaves. The two are often confused and only microscopic examination that reveals the chromosomes can distinguish for sure which is which.

The large leaves, to 10 inches long on the lower part of the plant, are alternate along the stem. Each is somewhat feather-shaped with lateral segments along the petiole also feather-shaped. The result is a lacy appearance, somewhat fern-like. They have a strong pungent odor.

The extensive horizontal root system is perennial.

Tiny white flowers are borne in small heads which form tight flat clusters which are slightly rounded on top. Clusters are 2 to 4 inches across. The flowers are mostly white, rarely pinkish. Rays of individual flowers are few – usually less than a dozen-surrounding the central disc. Rays are seldom more than one-sixth of an inch across.

The tiny seeds are flattened ovals with a slight margin.

Paiute Indians made a tea of yarrow for upset stomach. Many tribes treated wounds and burns with it. Meskwakis used it to bathe any part of the body that was ailing. The Winnebagos steeped the whole plant and treated earache with the resulting liquid.

Early settlers used a yarrow tea for fever. A poultice of the entire plant was used to treat skin rash. Leaves were gathered to make a treatment for various disorders of reproductive organs. Leaves were supposed to have a styptic quality, good for stopping nosebleed and easing toothache. Colds were also treated with yarrow tea. Washing the head regularly in a tea of dried yarrow was once thought to prevent baldness. In early medicine yarrow was thought to be especially effective in controlling hemorrhage in the abdominal and pelvic areas.

In ancient times, the European yarrow was also used in magic spells, in love charms – and even in place of hops for making beer.

...photograph by Alvin F. Bull

American waterlily: *Nymphaea tuberosa* Paine.

Other common names: castalia, pond lily, sweet white water-lily, water cabbage, water nymph.

Nymphaea: from Greek and Roman mythology, probably referring to the attractive and playful water nymphs of similar habitat.

Tuberosa: from Latin meaing "with tubers." Some authorities list *N. odorata* (meaning fragrant) as a separate species.

Waterlily family: *Nymphaeaceae.*

Found in the northern two-thirds of the state in ponds, shallow lakes, and slow-moving streams on rich bottom muds. May bloom from June until frost.

Large round leaves to one foot across float on the water surface above a submerged fleshy horizontal perennial rootstock. Leaves are dark green above; light green or purplish beneath. Smooth leaf margins have a single indentation to their center where the petiole is attached. Each petiole, usually has four main air channels which are easily visible when the petiole is cut in cross-section.

Showy white flowers with yellow centers may float on the water or may be held above it. Some are distinctly fragrant while others have only slight fragrance. This is a basis for separation into a different species, according to some authorites.

Numerous petals in the shape of narrow ovals may have pinkish cast and diminish in size toward the center. Four sepals are green outside, whitish inside. Flowers are to 6 inches across. One Indian legend tells that the waterlily was created from a falling star, an appropriate testimonial to the showy beauty of this flower.

Flowers of each *Nymphaea* species tend to open at a particular time each day. They follow the pattern for 3 or 4 days. Then they bend over (in shallow water) or coil down (in deeper water) so seeds ripen beneath the water surface. When mature in 6 to 10 weeks, the pods burst open and release seeds which float for several hours on the water surface. Action of the waves and wind then disperses seeds to other areas. This is nature's way of insuring survival of the species.

Early pioneers, but apparently not Indians, used the root as a treatment for dysentery, a gargle for sore throat, and a wash for sore eyes. Sometimes the root was powdered and combined with crushed seeds of flax or slippery elm to make a poultice for skin sores and other irriations. The leaves also served as a dressing for wounds and skin irritations.

Ojibwa Indians cooked the flowerbuds for food. The seeds, rich in digestible protein and oil, were also eaten by many tribes. So were the sturdy tubers which served as a substitute for potatoes.

Waterfowl and many other forms of wildlife feed on the American waterlily. *. . . photograph by Marlin Bowles*

Butter and eggs: *Linaria vulgaris* Hill.

Other common names: bacon and eggs, bread and butter, bread and cheese, bride-weed, chopped eggs, devil's flax, flax-weed, gallwort, impudent lawyer, rabbit flower, toad flax.

Linaria: from Latin *linum* for "flax", since some species resemble flax.

Vulgaris: from Latin for "common."

Snapdragon family: *Scrophulariaceae.*

Found throughout the state in open woodlands and fields, especially on sandy soils and usually in patches of many plants. Blooms June to October.

Slender erect stems grow to 3 feet tall, usually less. The leafy stem may be branched or solitary. Leaves are narrow, mostly somewhat pointed at both ends, and up to 1½ inches long. They occur alternately along the stem and without distinct petioles. A fine fuzz on the leaves may rub off easily. Both stems and leaves are a pale green color.

This vigorous perennial spreads freely by short underground stolons and tends to form large persistent patches. It is commonly regarded as a weed despite its attractive flowers.

Distinctive snapdragon-like flowers occur in compact spike-like clusters. Actually, it is not a true spike in that each flower has a short stem. Individual flowers, to 1¼ inches long, have the typical two-lobed upper lip and three-lobed lower lip of the snapdragon family. Middle lobe of the lower lip is the largest with a rounded palate-like projection that closes the throat of the flower. This palate is a distinct orange while other lips are a bright lemon yellow, sometimes white. The prominent nectar spur tends to be somewhat darker. Pollination is by insects.

The fruit capsule is oval in shape, less than a half inch long. It contains tiny black seeds with circular wings, resembling a miniature of the elm tree seed. The seeds are scattered by the wind as they are freed from the plant during the winter months.

Butter and eggs was used in early medicine as a treatment for jaundice. The entire plant was boiled as a laxative and tonic. Fumes were inhaled for bronchitis.

Juice of butter and eggs was once mixed with milk to serve as a homemade fly poison. An infusion of the leaves was once considered a spring tonic for winter-weary chickens.

The common name toadflax comes from the fact that this plant was a serious pest in European flax fields. It was introduced from Europe, but it is also a native of Asia.

A similar but more slender and closely related species, *L. canadenais* (L.) Dumont, has blue and white flowers. The entire plant and flowers tend to be somewhat smaller and more delicate than butter and eggs. Often a circle of new shoots grows up around the base of the plant.

Several species of this genus are annuals common in flower gardens of Europe. For some reason, they have found little favor in this country despite being colorful and easy to grow.

. . . photograph by Gus Hanuske

Dayflower: *Commelina communis* L.

Tradescantia virginiana

Other common names: Asiatic dayflower, wandering Jew.

Spiderwort family

Commelina: honoring the Commelin brothers, early Dutch botanists. Two were well known while the third died as a young man before making any significant contribution to the science. Linnaeus, in explaining the name, tells that the two conspicuous petals were for the famous brothers, the third small petal for the other brother.

Communis: from Latin meaning "common."

Spiderwort family: *Commelinaceae.*

Found growing in colonies throughout the state in shaded and protected areas, especially on moist rich soils of low woods or bottom lands and around dwellings. Flowers June to October.

Weak slender stems often trail along the ground, rooting at leaf attachments. Tips of the stem curve upward sometimes as much as 18 inches. Pieces of the stem cut or broken from the main plant readily develop their own new roots and start new plants.

Thick fleshy leaves, usually 3 to 5 inches long and 1½ inches wide, are lance-shaped with pointed tips. Veins are parallel and margins are smooth. The leaves, often without petioles, clasp the stem with a whitish membrane-like sheath which shows distinct green veins. This sheath is sometimes as much as an inch long. The root system of this unusual annual are slender and fibrous, but extensive enough to make it an aggressive competitor.

Distinctive showy flowers, usually a half inch or more across, cluster toward the tips of the up-curved stems. A large green keel-like sheath or bract unfolds and a flower emerges briefly on its own slender stalk, usually in the morning and for only part of one day. This is the basis for the common name dayflower. Two showy rounded blue petals give appearance of a two-petal flower. But a third smaller whitish petal below is nearly hidden by reproductive parts.

The fruit is a small two-celled capsule, each cell with two seeds.

The dayflower is used as a potherb in a number of countries of the world. Navajo Indians prepared a tea of the dayflower plant to be drunk by aging men and women to increase their potency. This Navajo belief was so firmly held that the same preparation was also fed to the tribe's breeding animals. There is no known record of such treatments having been effective.

Children sometimes crush the colorful petals to mark their skin with a pale blue stain as part of their play.

This native of Asia, despite its beauty, is often regarded as a weed. Species of dayflower native to United States include *C. erecta* L.

. . . photograph by Richard Lutz

Burdock: *Arctium minus* Schk.

Other common names: barbane, beggar button, burr barr, cockle button, cuckoo button, hard dock, stick button, wild rhubarb.

Arctium: from Greek *arctos* for "bear", referring to the rough flowerheads or the shaggy burs.

Minus: from Latin for "smaller", since other species are generally larger. At least one other species, *A. lappa* L. is also found in our area.

Daisy family: *Asteraceae (Compositae).*

Found throughout the state under a wide variety of conditions, especially in areas where some intensive use has been terminated. Flowers May to September.

The coarse much-branched stem is dark green, ridged, and strongly scented. The fleshy tap root of this biennial penetrates deep into the soil and lives over one winter. The first year of growth produces a basal rosette while the second produces the flowering growth.

The large leaves, to more than a foot long and nearly as wide, are generally roundish ovals more or less tapering to the tip – sometimes to the point of becoming almost triangular. Underside of the leaf tends to be covered with grayish hairs that are soft and woolly. Leaf margins may be smooth or coarsely toothed – and are often wavy.

Leaves are alternate and on long petioles. Lower leaves tend to be considerably more coarse than those higher on the stem.

A. minus Schk. grows to 5 feet tall and has leaves with hollow petioles. *A. lappa* L. is larger, to 10 feet tall, and less common. Its leaf petioles are solid with a distinct groove on the upper surface.

Tiny tubular flowers occur in heads. In *A. minus* Schk. these heads may measure three-fourths inch across and have short stems (or no stem at all). *A. lappa* L. heads grow to twice that size, are fewer in number, and have long stems. Both species have a rose purple color and shape much like the common thistle. A close look reveals surprising and delicate beauty in the flowers. Their base of hooked bracts forms a roundish bur which falls apart when ripe. As it approaches the ripened stage, the burs stick to clothing and animals. This is nature's way of insuring distribution of burdock seeds.

The root of the larger species, *A. lappa* L., is known as "gobo" in Japan where it is considered to rival salisfy as a vegetable. Burdock was introduced from Europe where young leaves, stems and roots were used as food. Iroquois and other tribes learned from early settlers to dry roots for use in soup.

Pioneers used the plant to treat gonorrhea, syphilis, gout, cancer, eye irritations, and skin problems.

A poultice of leaves was used for burns. A salve made from the root of *A. minus* Schk. was also used for skin infections. A tea of the roots is still used in parts of Appalachia for rheumatism and as a spring tonic.
. . photograph by Roger Landers

Starry campion: *Silene stellata* (L.) Ait.

Other common names: catchfly, widow's frill.

Silene: Probably from a mythological Greek god Silenus, the intoxicated foster father of Bacchus, who was described as slippery and being covered with foam. Others believe the origin of the name lies in the Greek word, *sialon*, meaning "saliva." Both are in reference to the sticky secretions covering the stems of some campions.

Stellata: from Latin meaning "starred."

Pink family: *Caryophyllaceae*.

Found throughout the state in dry upland woods and woodland slopes. Blooms July to September.

Stiff erect stems of this perennial grow to 3 feet tall from a much-branched crown. All except the lowest and uppermost leaves occur in whorls of four. The top and bottom leaves are paired opposite across the stem. Individual leaves are lance-shaped or sharp-tipped ovals to one inch across and 3 inches long. They have smooth margins and no petioles. Fine hairs on the underside give a downy appearance.

A deep taproot lives over the winter to make this plant a perennial.

Distinctive white flowers, each as much as three quarters of an inch across, occur in a loose head. The head is usually a single stalk, but may be branched. Each individual flower nods on its own short slender stalk or shares a stalk with another blossom.

The five white petals are united toward their bases into a bell shape. Toward their tips the individual petals flare outward. Each petal is deeply cut into numerous fine lobes. This produces a lacy fringe – the "starry" appearance from which the common name is derived. Origin of the campion portion of the name is obscure.

The petals protrude from a somewhat inflated bell-shaped calyx of five pointed sepals. The calyx may be slightly hairy and is not strongly veined – quite unlike that of its close relative bladder campion, *S. cucubalus* Wibel.

The dry seed capsule opens at the end, freeing numerous small bumpy seeds.

In early medicine, a poultice of starry campion roots was applied to infected sores and used as a treatment for aches, sprains, and open sores. This plant was called "wewep" by the Meskwaki tribe and "wawapin" by the Prairie Potawatomi tribe. Both used the roots as a poultice to dry up swellings that discharged pus.

Best known plants of this family are carnations and pinks, common in flower gardens. Starry campion itself is sometimes chosen for flower gardens.   *...photograph by Ruth Fagen*

Ground nut: *Apios americana* Medic.

Other common names: hopniss, Indian potato, potato bean, wild bean.

Apios: from Greek for "pear", referring to the shape of the tubers.

Americana: meaning "of America" since the species was found and studied on this continent. One other rare species is found in this country. Several other species are found in Asia.

Legume family: *Fabaceae (Leguminosae).*

Found throughout the state on damp rich soils along streams or woodland edges. Flowers in July and August.

This slender vining plant grows to 10 feet, climbing over other plants and twining extensively. Broken stems exude a milky juice. Alternate leaves divide into five or seven, rarely three or nine, leaflets arranged in pairs along a common petiole. One is at the end, accounting for the odd number. Each leaflet is rounded at the base, pointed at the tip, smooth at the margins, and up to 3 inches long.

The perennial roots form a necklace-like series of fleshy tubers, varying from one to 3 inches long.

The numerous pea-like flowers are brownish purple and have a strong fragrance. Each flower is perhaps a half inch long. They grow in short thick clusters along a slender flower stalk which arises from the leaf axils. The flower has a short but broad upper lip, slightly two-lobed, that is curved upward and outward. The lower lip is longer and with a distinct ridge or keel on its underside, typical of flowers of common peas.

The fruit is a straight slender pod about 3 inches long, resembling a bean pod and containing bean-like seeds. The fruit often fails to mature in normal seasons. So propogation is mostly by tubers from which new plants arise.

The groundnut was an important food plant for Indians and pioneers. Friendly Indians showed the New England pilgrims the value of ground nuts and how to use them. These became a major source of food during that first critical winter of 1620. But with obvious lack of appreciation, a law was passed in 1654 forbidding Indians to dig ground nuts on "English" land. First offense brought time in jail or the stocks. A second offense required a whipping.

Even Captain John Smith wrote in his journal of ground nuts "as big as eggs and as good as potatoes". Much later, the poet John Greenleaf Whittier wrote of "where the ground nut trails its vine" in *Barefoot Boy.*

The Meskwaki tribe called the plant "mukwo peniak" or bear potato and used it extensively as potatoes are used. Some Indians also used the bean-like seeds in much the same manner as peas.

The tubers are white and have a somewhat elastic texture. They were eaten raw, boiled, or roasted. Eaten raw, they are said to leave the feeling of a rubber coating on the teeth and lips. More often, they were cooked. For winter use, they were peeled, sliced, and dried for storage.

. . . photograph by John Schwegman

Virginia creeper: *Parthenocissus quinquefolia* (L.) Planch.

Other common names: five-finger ivy, five-leaf ivy, five-leafing, ghost grapes, woodbine.

Parthenocissus: from Greek meaning "virgin's ivy."

Quinquefoliia: from Latin meaning "five leaves", referring to the distinctive five leaflets of this plant.

Grape family: *Vitaceae.*

Found throughout the state climbing on trees (especially dead ones), fences, walls, and thickets. The species has adapted to a wide range of soils and other environmental conditions. Blooms July and August.

This slender-stemmed woody vine climbs to 20 feet or more by means of tendrils which end in little adhesive discs. These discs cling tenaciously to wood, bark, stone, or brick. Early tests by Charles Darwin (of evolution theory fame) showed that a single disc has a holding strength of as much as 2 pounds. The coiling tendency of the tendrils adds to the climbing and holding ability.

Leaves on long petioles are alternate along the stem. Each leaf, to 6 inches long, is usually divided into five leaflets – rarely three or seven. Margins are coarsely toothed. Each leaflet is an irregular narrow oval shape with a pointed tip. Their coloring is pale green beneath, darker on the upper side.

Flowers are small and inconspicuous in loose terminal clusters, sometimes of more than 200 flowers. Close examination reveals five spreading yellow-green to white petals.

The fruits are berries, each perhaps one-fourth inch in diameter, borne in sparse grape-like clusters. The berries ripen to a deep blue and usually contain two or three seeds. Stalks of the fruit cluster change from green to red as the fruit ripens. Fruits should not be eaten as they may be poisonous.

Though the flowers are not conspicuous, the foliage of this plant changes to a beautiful translucent scarlet in early autumn. As such, it often becomes one of the outstanding features of early autumn woodlands. The young leaves and branches often have an attractive purplish color before turning green with maturity. The attractive appearance and easy adaptation have led to wide use in landscaping – especially in parts of Europe. Virginia creeper does not have the toxic character of poison ivy.

Chippewa Indians used the stem, especially the soft layer next to the bark, to make a tea for beverage purposes. Omaha and Ponca Indians called the plant a term meaning "ghost grapes" and carefully avoided it.

Meskwaki and Potawatomi Indians boiled the roots to make a tea for treating diarrhea.

Green leaves and berries have been used for fever and to make a tea to treat bladder troubles.

. . . photograph by Herbert H. Hadow

Other common names: Canada lily, Michigan lily, tiger lily, Turk's cap lily, wood lily.

Lilium: the classical Latin name for lilies, probably originating in ancient Greek or Persian usage.

Species: four or five species occur as natives in the state. Some garden flowers commonly called lilies are members of the same family, but not of this genus.

Lily family: *Liliaceae*

Found throughout the state in open woods, low areas, and prairie swales. Plants often cluster in large groups where soil is moist to wet. Blooms mostly in July and August.

These plants grow to 5 to 6 feet tall from perennial scaly rootstocks or bulbs. Leaves, usually less than 6 inches long, occur in whorls or alternate along the stem. The sword-shaped leaves have parallel veins and smooth margins. The stems often branch at the tip to form additional flower stalks.

The flowers are large and colorful – commonly an orange-red but sometimes white or yellow. Dark spots on the inside of the six petals are typical of true lilies. Individual flowers are often 3 inches across. They are somewhat bell-shaped, usually nodding. The slender pointed petals may be strongly curved back so much that their tips almost touch. Long pistils and stamens protrude from the center of the flower.

The common Michigan lily(*L. Michiganense* Farw.) is often mistaken for Turk's cap lily (*L. superbum* L.). But Turk's cap, found mostly in more eastern states, has a pronounced green streak inside of each petal. This green forms a distinct star when petals are viewed together in a complete flower.

Tiger lily (*L. tigrinum* L.) closely resembles these two except that its leaves are alternate along the stem instead of in whorls. Another distinguishing feature is a smooth shiny black "berry" generally present in leaf axils. This species is an introduction from Asia and has escaped to grow wild.

The smaller wood lily (*L. philadelphicum* L.) grows on the more acid soils of woodlands and prairies, mostly in the northern half of the state. It usually stands less than 3 feet tall and holds its flower facing upward rather than nodding.

Seeds of the lily genus are borne in dry capsules with three compartments. Two rows of small seeds are densely packed in each compartment.

Bulbs of Canada lily (*L. canadense* L.) were cooked or used to thicken soup by Indians of several tribes. This was probably true of other lily species, too. Some considered a tea made from the bulbs useful for treating snakebite. Sometimes the flower of the tiger lily was chewed to a paste for treating spider bites.

Another genus in the same family is *Hemerocallus*. It has lily-like flowers borne on leafless flower stalks. The leaves are long and narrow. This is a European genus which has escaped from early flower gardens.   *. . . photograph by Richard Lutz*

American lotus: *Nelumbo lutea* (Willd.) Pers.

Other common names: duck acorn, great yellow water lily, rattlenut, water chinquapin, waternut, wankapin, yackeynut, yankapin.

Nelumbo: a word of Ceylonese origin for the Asian lotus.

Lutea: from Latin for "yellow" from the color of the large and showy flower.

Water lily family: *Nymphaeaceae.*

Found throughout the state in still or slow-moving waters with rich bottom muds. Blooms July to September.

Large round leaves as much as 2 feet in diameter are attached at the center to the petiole. Their smooth margins are upturned to resemble a shallow circular pan. Prominent veins radiate from the center to the outer edge, usually branching once or twice toward the leaf margin. Leaves may be held a foot or more above the water, or may float on the water surface.

The horizontal perennial rootstock may be as long as 50 feet. In the fall, numerous tuberous enlargements store starch to provide nourishment for early growth the following spring.

Pale yellow sweet-scented flowers resembling water lilies are held above the water. They are large, often 8 inches across. Each flower has several rows of petals and sepals. The sepals closely resemble petals in appearance. An elevated receptable stands in the center of the flower. As seeds develop, this funnel-shaped receptacle expands to as much as 5 inches across and becomes woody. Its flat top is pitted, with each pit holding a spherical acorn-like seed perhaps a half inch in diameter. There may be as many as 25 to 30 seeds per receptacle. Individual seeds may remain dormant for many decades before sprouting -- perhaps as long as 1000 years.

The seeds have long been an important source of food for Indians in the eastern half of this country. Eaten when half ripe, their taste resembles chestnuts. Ripe seeds were boiled or roasted.

Growing tips and tubers along the underwater rootstock were prepared for food by boiling or roasting. Their flavor reminds one of yams or sweet potatoes. For storage, Indians cut these banana-like tubers crosswise into small sections and strung them on a basswood string. Once dried, they could be stored in a dry place until needed. Then they were soaked and cooked with meat, corn, or beans. As such, they served as an important winter food supply for many tribes.

As long as 400 years ago, Indians cultivated the American lotus on the Cumberland and Tennessee Rivers. Longtime Amana, Iowa, residents will remember groups of Indians camping beside the old Amana millpond while squaws waded waist-deep in chilly autumn waters to harvest the tubers.

Many kinds of birds and wild animals also feed on this plant.

. . . photograph by Ruth Fagen

Cardinal flower: *Lobelia cardinalis* L.

Other common names: red lobelia

Lobelia: in honor of the 16th century Flemish herbalist, Mattias de l'Obel.

Cardinalis: from Latin meaning "of a cardinal" for the brilliant red color of the flower or "of the Cardinal" from the color and shape of the flower which bears some resemblance to the Cardinal's miter or cap.

Bluebell family *Campanulaceae.* (Some botanists prefer to place the lobelias in their own family named *Lobeliaceae.*)

Found throughout the state on rich soils of open woodlands along streams and other low moist areas. Blooms July through September.

An erect leafy stem, usually without branches, grows to 4½ feet high. Numerous lance-shaped leaves are alternate along the smooth stem. The leaves grow to 6 inches long on the lower stem, seldom to more than 2 inches on the upper stem. They are usually three or four times longer than wide. Lower leaves have short petioles; upper leaves have none. A basal rosette of leaves is typical. The leaves are dark green with finely-toothed margins. The plant parts contain a milky juice which is considered poisonous – or at least toxic to some degree.

The coarsely fibrous perennial root system is extensive. It develops slender offshoots from which new plants arise.

The showy flowers add a flash of brilliant crimson to woodlands in late summer and early autumn. Cardinal flower is one of the most striking of all the flowers found in nature's woodlands. Numerous flowers crowd the top of the stem to form a dense terminal spike. Lower flowers may appear on short stalks in the axils of upper leaves. Individual flowers, about an inch long, have two lips divided nearly to the base.

The upper lip has two pointed lobes which flare upward. The lower lip has three pointed lobes which curve downward. A bundle of five long stamens (male flower parts) protrudes from the center of the flower. A "beard" or brush at the end of the stamens is a glistening white – a striking feature when the flower is given close examination. The split lower lip with descending lobes provides an unstable landing pad for the larger bees so the smaller species are more important for pollination. Hummingbirds also assist in pollination.

The fruit is a capsule with two cavities, each containing many small seeds.

This species was used in early medicine, probably more or less interchangeably with other *Lobelia* species. Early reports tell of use to treat syphilis and internal parasites. Juice of the plant is poisonous – similar to nicotine.

Meskwaki Indians crushed the entire plant for a ceremonial "tobacco." It was not for smoking. But to ward off an approaching storm, some of this tobacco was thrown to the winds. It was also scattered over a grave as the final ceremonial rite.

Roots were also used as a love charm.

. . . photograph by W. K. Hollinsworth

Cup plant: *Silphium perfoliatum* L.

Other common names: carpenter weed, cup rosin weed, Indian cup, ragged cup, rosin weed.

Silphium: from Greek, the ancient name of a resinous African plant. The name was later transferred to this genus probably because of the resinous juices of some species.

Perfoliatum: from Latin for "through the leaf" referring to the base of the leaf surrounding the stem.

Daisy family: *Asteraceae (Compositae).*

Found throughout the state on rich, medium-to-wet soils of open woodlands and meadows. Blooms July to September.

This coarse tall perennial grows to 8 feet high. Its smooth erect stem is square – four angled – from which the common name carpenter weed originates. It may be single or branched. Leaves are opposite. Larger lower ones have winged petioles and may be as much as 12 inches long and 8 inches wide. On the upper part of the plant, the paired leaves are smaller and without petioles. These join around the stem to form shallow cups which catch rainwater. The leaves are pointed, somewhat triangular in shape. They are thin yet rough on both sides. Margins have coarse widely spaced teeth.

Showy yellow flowerheads, to 3 inches across, have a center disc and 20 to 30 slender petal-like ray flowers. Each ray flower may produce a small winged seed with a slender oblong shape. Only close examination reveals the true complexity of these colorful flowers.

Multiple flowers, each on a separate stalk, arise from the top leaf axil of the main stem or branch.

Rain water collected in the "cups" served Indians as emergency drinking water, especially when they were on trips into unfamiliar territory. Many tribes made extensive use of roots to brew a tea for treating hemorrhage of lungs, rheumatism, excessive menstrual flow, fever, vomiting during pregnancy, and numerous other ailments. Early settlers used the cup plant for similar purposes.

The plant was also burned to produce a smudge for treating colds and neuralgia. The Chippewas dried and pounded the root before making it into a compress for application to bleeding wounds.

This plant was so highly regarded among Indian medicine men that Wisconsin tribes even journeyed to Iowa to procure roots for transplanting to their primitive "gardens" of medicinal plants.

A closely related species of the prairie, *S. laciniatum* L. or compass plant, served as a source of chewing gum for the Omaha Indians. When the flowering head was removed, the resinous juices hardened to provide the gummy mass suitable for chewing. The same thing may have been tried with the cup plant although its juices are slightly less resinous.

. . . photograph by William Welker

False foxglove: *Gerardia grandiflora*, Benth.

Other common names: Oak leech.

Gerardia: in honor of John Gerard, a prominent early English horticulturist. (Some authorities prefer *Aureolaria* as the name for this genus.)

Grandiflora: from Latin for "large flower." A few other species are also found sparingly in the state.

Snapdragon family: *Scrophulariaceae.*

Found throughout the state on acid soils of open woodlands. Rather dry and rocky woodlands or sandy thickets are preferred. May be partially parasitic on roots of oak trees. The *grandiflora* species is frequent only in the western part of the state. Blooms from July to September.

The false foxgloves are tall plants with many opposite leaves. *G. flava* L., to 5 feet high, has a smooth purplish stem that is usually branched toward the top. Its stem has a powdery appearance. Its leaves are long ovals so deeply cleft that they may appear as smaller leaflets along the central vein. *G. grandiflora* Benth., to 4½ feet high, has a downy stem with spreading branches toward the top. Leaves of both species are similar and have short petioles. *G. pedicularia* Benth., is annual, while the other two are perennial. This annual to 8 feet tall, has a much-branched stem with sticky hairs. Its leaves, so extensively cleft they appear fern-like, have longer petioles.

The large showy false foxglove flowers are lemon-yellow to golden elongated bells with five petals joined for most of their length. The petals tend to be slightly irregular. They have the familiar waxy sheen of buttercups. The petals are based in a five-lobed green calyx. Calyx lobes are longer than the calyx tube. The lobes of some species are coarsely toothed, sometimes to the point of resembling the leaves.

Single flowers on individual flower stalks arise from axils of the upper leaves which are actually reduced to bracts. The flowers and their bracts often crowd along the upper stem to form a spike-like raceme. *G. flava* L. flowers are generally less than 2 inches long. Those of *G. grandiflora* Benth. are slightly larger. Flowers of *G. pedicularia* L. are smaller, to 1½ inch long and often tinged with purple.

The tiny seeds of *G. pedicularia* L. are wingless while those of the other two species have distinctly winged margins. The dry seed capsules are mostly less than a half inch long.

No medicinal or food uses by Indians or pioneers are known.

The *Gerardia* species are generally considered semi-parasitic. They often fasten themselves firmly to a host plant, commonly the roots of oak trees. But their own green leaves manufacture most of the food for the plants. They seem to do no harm to the host trees.   *...photograph by Kitty Kohout*

Blue lobelia: *Lobelia siphilitica* L.

Other common names: blue cardinal flower, great blue lobelia.

Lobelia: in honor of a 16th century Flemish herbalist, Matthias de l'Obel.

Siphilitica: because it was once thought to be a cure for syphillis.

Bluebell family: *Campanulaceae.* (Some botanists prefer to place the lobelias in their own family named *Lobeliaceae.*)

Found throughout the state in open woodlands along streams and in low moist areas. Flowers July to September.

The blue lobelia produces a single erect leafy stem arising to 5 feet from a basal rosette of long narrowed-oval leaves. Alternate leaves crowded along the coarse stem are of similar shape but are pointed at the tip. They have toothed margins and tiny stiff hairs on the upper side. Size varies from 2 to 6 inches long with the smaller leaves toward the top. Lower leaves have short petioles; upper leaves are without petioles. Juice of the plant is milky and somewhat poisonous. The perennial root system is coarsely fibrous and white.

Light blue flowers to an inch long grow from the axils of upper leaves. The upper lip of the flower has two erect and slightly diverging lobes that are divided to their base. Through this slit emerges a curved column consisting of the stamens (male flower parts) joined in a ring around the style (female flower part). Close examination shows that two of the stamens are tipped with anthers that are tufted or hairy. These unique characteristics are typical of the *Lobelia* genus.

The lower lip has three spreading lobes and is striped with white. Flowers and small leaves crowd together on the upper stem to appear almost as a flower spike.

Some Indians believed this plant to be a secret cure for syphilis. The "secret" was purchased from the Indians and taken to Europe where it failed to perform to expectation. The Indians did not disclose that they used it in combination with May apple root plus bark of wild cherry and afterward dusted open sores with powdered bark of New Jersey tea. There seems little reason for the Indian treatment to have effected a cure, either.

Other Indians used blue lobelia as a love potion by secretly placing finely ground root powder in the food of an arguing couple.

The flowers were sometimes used to produce an inhalant for catarrh.

Lobelia inflata L., a closely related species sometimes called Indian tobacco, is still used in parts of Appalachia to treat respiratory troubles. It also yields lobeline sulfate which is used in antismoking products. While Indians were said to have chewed and smoked this plant as a tobacco substitute, this seems unlikely because of the poisonous nature of the plant. It seems more logical that its use was as a ceremonial "tobacco" alone or in combination with other plants.

The lobelias, have been considered a cure for most diseases of pioneers at one time or another. ... *photograph by Roger Landers*

Jewelweed: *Impatiens biflora* Walt.,

Other common names: balsam, celandine, impatience, kicking colt, orange snapweed, quick-in-the-hand, silver slipper, snapdragon, solentine, speckled jewels, touch-me-not, weather cock, yellow snapweed.

Impatiens: from Latin for "impatient", referring to the explosive action of the fruit which distributes the seed.

Biflora: from Latin for "two flowered." (Some botanists prefer *capensis* referring to the Cape of Good Hope. The botanist who gave it this name thought the plant was found there originally, but was in error.) A yellow flowered species, *I. pallida* Nutt. (from Latin meaning "pale"), is less common.

Tough-me-not family: *Balsaminaceae.*

Found throughout the state in damp, low woodlands, especially near streams and swampy areas. Blooms July to September.

Annual plants of this species grow to 5 feet tall. The branched stems are weak and watery. Color is pale green, with a translucent look. Stem joints are enlarged. Leaves are thin and pale, blusish-green in color. They are oval to egg-shaped with coarsely toothed margins. They are alternate along the stem and up to 3½ inches in length with petioles often as long as the leaf. Leaves of the yellow-flowered variety (*I. pallida* Nutt.) are similar but narrower. Dew often accumulates in glistening droplets on the leaves giving rise to the name jewelweed.

Flowers are usually orange with dots of reddish brown. They may also be pale yellow (*I. pallida* Nutt.), rarely white. Flowers, to 1¼ inches long, appear singly or in loose clusters. The flower has a curious shape – somewhat like a funnel partially closed at the larger end. The smaller end is a curved spur holding nectar. Bees may disapper into the flower as they search for nectar. A slender flower stalk curves from the leaf axil and attaches to the center of the funnel, suspending the flower like a pendant.

The fruit is a slender capsule perhaps an inch long, which shrinks in drying. As it splits, seeds are scattered in all directions as if propelled by a small explosion. Often the splitting occurs when the fruit is touched. The seeds taste delicious – like butternuts – but may be hard to catch.

Potawatomi Indians applied the juice of the jewelweed to relieve the itch of poison ivy. So did pioneers. A pulp of leaves and stems provided treatment for other skin problems among the Omahas and many other tribes. The Blackfoot Indians included roots in their preparations for similar uses.

In pioneer folk medicine, the leaves were sometimes made into a general tonic. Fresh juice squeezed from the plant was rubbed on an aching forehead to ease the pain.

Even today, juice of the jewelweed is used to relieve the burning sensation from touching stinging nettle. These two plants are often found in the same habitat.

Livestock have been poisoned by eating excessively of the fresh green plants.   *...photograph by Roger Landers*

Other common names: boneset, gravel root, hempweed, jopi root, jopi weed, kidney root, king-of-the-meadow, marsh milkweed, motherwort, queen-of-the-meadow, quillwort, skunk weed, stink weed, trumpet weed, and others.

Eupatorium: from Greek meaning "good father," in honor of Mithridates Eupator (132-63 B.C.) who is said to have used a species of this genus in medical practice.

Purpureum: from Latin for "purple."

Daisy family: *Asteraceae (Compositae).*

Found throughout the state at the edge of wet places where woodlands open into wet thickets and marshes. Blooms July to September.

The slender erect stem, branched or unbranched, grows to 10 feet tall. It is essentially round, sometimes ridged, and solid – not hollow as in some related species. The green of the stem may be tinged with purple shading to a deep purple at the joints.

Large thinnish leaves are narrow pointed ovals as much as a foot long and 3 inches wide. They are opposite, or often in whorls of three or four, sometimes more. Margins are sharply saw-toothed. Veins are conspicuous on the underside. The petioles are relatively short but longer than for most related species. When crushed or drying, the leaves and stem give off a sweetish vanilla odor. The roots of this perennial are coarse, tough, and fibrous.

Tiny fragrant flower heads mass in large dome-like clusters as much as 6 or more inches across. A number of smaller branches make up the cluster. Each branch contains several flower heads in the shape of slender cylinders. The cylindrical flower head contains three to seven tiny flowers, each perhaps three-eighths inch across. Individual flowers may be creamy white, pale pink, or pale lilac. They have short ray petals plus long stamens (male flower parts) and long pistils (females flower parts) which give the characteristic fuzzy appearance to the Joe Pye weed flower cluster.

Seed heads often persist into winter releasing tiny five-angled seeds with tufts of hair to be distributed by the wind.

Legend tells that Joe Pye, an Indian herb doctor of the Massachusetts Bay Colony, used this plant to cure fevers. The plant obtained its common name from this Indian.

The plant is still used in parts of Appalachia to treat urinary disorders. Earlier, Iroquois Indians had done the same.

Chippewa Indian mothers bathed fretful children in a tea made from this plant to bring restful sleep. This was also thought to strengthen the child. A Meskwaki brave nibbled leaves of the Joe Pye weed to insure success when wooing his choice of tribal maidens.

A similar species, *E. maculatum* L., is also commonly called Joe Pye weed. The flower cluster of this species is flat-topped while that of *E. purpureum* is more round topped.

. . . photograph by Roger Landers

Partridge pea: *Chamaecrista fasciculata* Greene.

Other common names: golden cassia, large-flowered sensitive pea, prairie senna, senna pea, wild sensitive plant.

Chamaecrista: from Greek meaning "low crest."

Fasciculata: from Latin meaning "grouped together in bundles," probably referring to the drooping flower parts.

Legume family: *Fabaceae (Leguminosae).*

Found throughout the state on dry sandy soils, especially along roadsides and other places where natural vegetation has been disturbed. This sun-loving plant occurs mostly in prairies and in woodland edges. Blooms July to September.

This annual may grow spreading or erect to 2½ feet tall. Its main stem is branched but branches are usually simple – without further branching. The stem may be either smooth or finely hairy.

Large compound leaves grow alternate along the branches. Each leaf has as many as 15 pairs of oval leaflets, less than an inch long and attached without individual petioles to the midrib. The resulting leaf resembles that of the related locust tree (same family). There is no odd-numbered leaflet at the end of the mid-rib.

Each leaflet is tipped with a tiny bristle. Leaf segments fold along the mid-rib like falling dominoes when touched. This, of course, is the basis for the word "sensitive" in some of the common names. The leaves fold in a similar manner at night and re-open in the morning.

Two to four flowers on separate slender stalks arise from axils of the upper leaves. They are usually canary yellow, but may be white. A patch of purple may occur near the base of each petal. Flowers are showy and large – often an inch or more across. The five petals are unequal. The lower petal and one of the lateral ones are larger than the other three. An upper petal is usually attached inside of the others. Five narrow green sepals are as long as the petals. Six drooping purple anthers (male flower parts) are a prominent feature of this flower.

The fruit is a hairy flattish pod typical of legumes. It may measure as much as 2 inches long and nearly one-fourth inch wide. The small brown seeds within the pod may number as many as a dozen. They are a favorite food of partridges, quail, and other birds.

Related species have been used in Old World medicine. The drug senna comes from several species native to Egypt and Arabia. Despite this, any uses of partridge pea by American Indians and pioneers are not known. The foliage is considered toxic to livestock by some authorities.

. . . photograph by John Schwegman

Woodland sunflower: *Helianthus strumosus* L.

Other common names: pale-leaved wood sunflower.

Helianthus: from Greek *helios* for "sun" and *anthos* for "flower", hence "sunflower" because heads of this genus tend to be turned with the sun each day.

Strumosus: from Latin meaning "swelling" or "tumor" referring to the swollen base of the stiff sharp hairs on this species, especially on the upper side of the leaves.

Daisy family: *Asteraceae (Compositae).*

Found mostly in the northern part of the state in dry open upland woods, thickets and woodland edges. Blooms July to Sept.

The stout erect stem, branched toward the top, grows to 7 or more feet tall. The main stem is smooth, but the branches are usually hairy.

The leaves are thick, roughened by stiff hairs above and often by finer hairs beneath. The underside is whitish or grayish in color. The leaves are shaped as narrow pointed ovals, sometimes with shallow teeth on the margins. They are carried on slender-based petioles – alternate along the main stem and usually opposite on the branches. They are usually less than 8 inches long and 2½ inches wide.

The perennial root system is a long slender, and sometimes branched, rhizome that may have tuberous swellings.

Flowerheads occur in loose clusters at the tips of the stem branches. The yellow center disk, as much as an inch across, is surrounded by five to 15 brilliant yellow petal-like rays. Total flowerhead is usually as much as 2½ to 4 inches across.

The seeds, borne in the central disk, are thick flat ovals with a smooth surface.

Indians used seeds for food – ground into a powder or roasted, and as a source of oil. Oil released by boiling the seeds in water rose to the surface when the water cooled and was skimmed off for use in cooking.

The Meskwaki and Prairie Pottawatomi tribes made a tea of roots for various lung troubles. Ojibwas made extensive food and medicinal use of sunflowers.

Since species of sunflower are numerous and may hybridize, exact species used is often in doubt. It seems likely that several species were involved, probably on an interchangeable basis. Various other uses have included tobacco substitute, coffee substitute, fiber for cords, fly control, yellow dye (from petals), and many others.

An annual sunflower, *H. annuus*, was being cultivated by Indians long before white men arrived in this hemisphere. That species is the origin of the present commercial sunflower crop which is expanding rapidly in several parts of the world.

. . . photograph by Jane Eddy

Other common names: balmony, bitter herb, codhead, fish mouth, shellflower, snakehead, snake mouth, turtlebloom, white turtlehead.

Chelone: from Greek for "tortoise" since the flower resembles the head of a tortoise.

Glabra: from Latin meaning "smooth" referring to the lack of hairs or other texture on the leaves and stems.

Snapdragon family: *Scrophulariaceae.*

Found throughout the state, mostly along streams and in wet thickets or bottom woodlands. Blooms July to September.

A single smooth squarish stem arises from a creeping perennial rootstock, and grows to 3 feet tall. Short lateral branches may appear toward the top of the stem.

Smooth dark green leaves from 2 to 6½ inches long and on short winged petioles are paired opposite along the stem and branches. The leaves are long and narrow, with pointed tips. Veining is prominent and margins are sharply toothed. The shape of the leaves may be quite variable with this species. The leaves may be slightly hairy, but this also varies within the species.

The flowers, as the common name indicates, are shaped somewhat like the head of a turtle with its mouth open. The upper lip is broad and arching. The lower lip is three lobed with the outer lobes larger than the middle one. This lower lip is woolly in the throat of the flower. The color is whitish to yellow-green, sometimes tinged with pink. The flowers are usually an inch to one and a half inches long.

The flowers usually crowd along a dense terminal spike. At times, a few additional flowers may occur in the axils of upper leaves. Close examination shows five stamens (male flower parts) one of which is smaller than the other four and is sterile.

When a bumblebee enters the flower and disappears inside after nectar, his movements and the resulting vibration of the flower give the appearance that the bee is being chewed up by the turtlehead blossom.

The fruit is an oval capsule about a half inch long. Each of its two cells contains many small winged seeds.

This plant provided a favorite tonic and laxative for several tribes of Indians despite its bitter taste. Pioneers used leaves of turtlehead as a tonic and as a treatment for jaundice, constipation, and internal parasites. Leaves were also made into an ointment to relieve itching and inflammations.

Varieties of this species are often available from dealers in wildflower seeds and plants.

A less common species with rose-purple flowers, *C. obliqua* L. is known as pink turtlehead.   . . . *photograph by Ruth Fagen*

Horsemint: *Monarda fistulosa* L.

Other common names: bee balm, wild bergamot

Monarda: in honor of a Spanish physician and botanist, Nicolas Monardes, who wrote widely in the 16th centruy about medicinal and otherwise useful plants of the new world.

Fistulosa: from Latin meaning "like a reed or pipe" in reference to individual flowers.

Mint family: *Lamiaceae (Labiatae).*

Found throughout the state, often in dense colonies on rich soils of open woods, roadsides, and old pastures. Flowers July to September.

The sturdy square stem, typical of the mint family, grows erect to about 5 feet tall. It is usually branched and somewhat hairy toward the top. Leaves on short petioles are opposite. Each pair is at right angles to the adjacent pair. Individual leaves are somewhat oval in shape but narrowing and pointed toward the tip. Margins are unevenly toothed.

Both leaves and stem have a minty aroma and a gray-green color that may be tinged with purple. These characteristics are typical of the mints. The aroma lasts into the winter long after the foliage has died.

The perennial root system is a clump of fibrous rootlets and rhizomes.

Individual flowers are slender pink to lavender tubes, each with a distinct lip or lobe. These inch-long tubes cluster together in dense but ragged heads that may be 1½ inches across. Stamens protrude from the tubes, adding to the ragged appearance.

At least one other *Monarda* species is native to the state. It is shorter with flowers of light yellow spotted with purple dots. Still another called oswego tea, *M. didyma* L., is a native of eastern U.S. which has escaped from garden plantings in our area. Its beautiful crimson flower may brighten woodlands in late summer.

Winnebago Indians secured an oil, by boiling leaves, to use in treating pimples and similar skin eruptions. The Blackfoot tribe applied boiled leaves for the same purpose. Meskwaki Indians used the plant in a mixture to cure colds. Navajos made a tea of horsemint to treat fevers, sore throat, colds, and headache. So did early pioneers.

Other Indians used a warm liquid from the boiled leaves to bathe a patient suffering from chills. The aromatic dried herb was boiled to produce vapors for bronchial ailments. A tea of the roots was used to treat stomach disorders.

The mint family, with small glands which secrete the characteristic aromatic and volatile oil, has furnished many herbs and flavorings used by mankind. Among those still being used are marjoram, rosemary, peppermint, spearmint, horehound, thyme, sage, lavender, catnip, hyssop, and pennyroyal.

. . . photograph by Richard F. Trump

Trumpet vine: *Campsis radicans* (L.) Şeem.

Other common names: cow itch, devil's shoelace, trumpet ash, trumpet creeper, trumpet flower.

Campsis: from Greek meaning generally "curved" referring to the curved stamens.

Radicans: from Latin meaning "rooting" in reference to the aerial rootlets formed along the stem.

Bignonia family: *Bignoniaceae.*

Found throughout the state, but only as an infrequent escape from domestic planting in the northern part which is beyond its natural range. It generally favors low woods and thickets. Blooms July to September.

The stem is an agressive vine that becomes woody with age. It grows to as much as 40 feet, trailing over bushes, thickets, fences, trees and telephone poles. Aerial rootlets, not tendrils, help it climb. The perennial root system is extensive.

The leaves, usually 8 to 15 inches long over all, have seven, nine, or eleven leaflets on short stems along the main petiole. They are opposite except for one at the tip. The leaflets are sharply pointed egg shapes perhaps 3 inches long and with toothed margins. The compound leaves are arranged opposite along the stem.

The showy flowers are large funnel shapes about 2½ inches long and 1½ inches across. Their orange to scarlet color is almost as striking as their size. They occur in short-stalked clusters of fewer than 10 blossoms. Reproductive parts of the flower are shorter than the "funnel." The flaring outer part of the funnel has five shallow lobes.

The seed pods are cigar-shaped capsules 4 to 6 inches long. Each is carried on its own short stalk. The capsule is divided lengthwise into two segments. Each segment is ridged at the edges where it joins its companion segment. The seeds, with broad lateral wings, are arranged in several rows within the pods.

No medical or food uses of *Campsis radicans* by Indians or pioneers are known. Many early settlers in our area used trumpet vine for landscaping because of its showy flowers. Farther south, it may become so aggressive that it is regarded as serious weed.

When the famous James Audubon painted the ruby-throated hummingbirds, he showed then hovering near flowers of the trumpet vine.

Some people are allergic to this species and develop a rash somewhat like that from poison ivy from contact.

. . . photograph by John Schwegman

Bootjack: *Bidens* many species L.

Other common names: beggar ticks, bur marigold, devil's pitchfork, Spanish needles, stick-tights, tickseed sunflower.

Bidens: from Latin, meaning "two-toothed", referring to the shape of the fruits.

Species: of several species in the state, *B. vulgata* Greene, *B. cernua* L. and *B. frondosa* L. are among the more common.

Daisy family: *Asteraceae (Compositae).*

Found throughout the state on wet soils, sometimes covering the entire lower part of open valleys and wide waterways. *B. frondosa* L. is frequent on streambanks and moist areas where the soil has been disturbed. *B. cernua* L. is common in and near marshes. Blooms July to frost.

Erect stems of various species may be branched and range in height from a few inches to more than 6 feet. Leaves are opposite, on long petioles in most species. Some are divided into leaflets. Leaves, or leaflets, are more or less lance shaped with toothed margins.

B. cernua L. has a much branched stem that grows to more than 6 feet. Larger plants may be more or less reclining with new roots starting where stems touch the soil. Leaves of this species are mostly without petioles. Heads are erect during flowering, nodding in the fruit stage.

B. frondosa L. grows to 3 feet tall on slender leafy stems. Subdivisions of the leaf have petioles in this species. *B. vulgata* Greene is quite similar.

Crushed plant parts of *Bidens* species have a disagreeable odor.

Golden flowers of various species range from a half inch to 1½ inches across. Numerous flowers grow in heads at tips of upper branches. Most are daisy-like with showy rays. Some are without rays. Most of the *Bidens* species have leaf-like bracts at the base of the flowerhead. Despite the colorful flowers, the *Bidens* species are considered bothersome weeds.

The fruits of *B. frondosa* L. are shaped like miniature boot jacks with two sharp arms. Those of *B. cernua* L. have four arms. These arms, called awns, have tiny barbs which hold the seeds tenaciously to clothes or animals. This is nature's way of transporting seeds to new areas. The *Bidens* species are probably more noted for the nuisance of the clinging seeds than for their beautiful flowers. This is another of nature's amazing, and this time not so pleasant, feats.

Some African natives use the leaves of certain species as salad greens. But the plant has had no extensive food or medicinal uses in this country, perhaps because of the unpleasant odor.

Another less common genus, *Coreopsis*, is often confused with *Bidens*. Its foliage, flowers, and fruits are quite similar. The yellow rays of *Coreopsis* usually number eight and often are notched or toothed at their tips. ...*photograph by Bruce Plum*

Arrowhead: *Sagittaria latifolia* Willd.

Other common names: broadleaf arrowhead, duck potato, Indian onion, katniss, swamp potato, swan potato, tule potato, wapatoo, water nut.

Sagittaria: From Latin meaning "of an arrow", referring to the arrowhead shape of the leaf.

Latifolia: From Latin meaning "wide or broad leaf."

Water plantain family: *Alismataceae (Alismaceae).*

Found throughout the state in wet bottom lands, marshes, and edges of shallow water in ponds and slow moving water. Blooms from July to October.

As its name implies, this plant is distinguished by its dark green leaves in the shape of broad arrowheads. Leaves, 2 to 8 inches long, occur mostly above the water level on petioles to 3 feet long. In deeper water leaves may become narrower – sometimes almost grass-like. Plant juices are distinctly milky.

The perennial root system has long runners which produce white potato-size tubers in late summer. Tubers, typically twice as long as broad, end in a pointed tip.

Attractive flowers to 1¾ inches across appear in whorls of two to five, mostly three, around erect spike-like flower stalks. Flower parts occur in threes – three petals and three sepals. Petals are rounded, usually with a slight indentation.

In most cases, the smaller upper flowers bear pollen while the larger lower flowers are the seed producers. Individual seeds, about one-eighth of an inch across, develop in spherical clusters. These clusters range from a half to 1½ inches across.

Tubers of arrowhead provided a major food source for many Indian tribes. As such, they were often an important commodity in trade between tribes. Some Indians sliced the boiled tubers and strung the pieces on basswood cords to dry in the sun. Once thoroughly dried, the slices stored easily and became a major winter food supply. The potato-like tubers were mostly boiled or roasted. When cooked, they tend to lose their slightly bitter taste and take on the flavor of water chestnuts.

Early explorers often depended on arrowhead tubers for food. Lewis and Clark ate the tubers and referred to them as "wapatoo" in their journal records. Wapatoo was perhaps the most common name applied to this species by Indians throughout the west.

Indian women harvested tubers by entering the chilly autumn water, supporting themselves by a hold on a canoe, and forcing tubers loose with their toes. Thus freed, the tubers floated to the surface where they could be collected and tossed into a canoe. When a storage cache of a muskrat colony could be found, tubers were stolen – or "traded" by replacing with a more plentiful food to avoid angering whatever powers were supposed to look after the welfare of muskrats.

Both fruits and tubers are food to various species of waterfowl.

. . . photograph by Ruth Fagen

Rose mallow: *Hibiscus militaris* Cav.

Other common names: halberd mallow, mallow rose, swamp mallow, water mallow.

Hibiscus: old Greek and Latin name for a kind of large mallow.

Militaris: from Latin meaning "soldierly", probably for the erect and imposing appearance of the plant. Or perhaps for the halberd shape of the leaves.

Mallow family: *Malvaceae.*

Found mostly in the southern part of the state in wooded bottomlands where soils are continuously wet and swampy. It sometimes occurs in extensive colonies. Blooms July to October.

Clusters of smooth, soft, pithy stems grow to 7 feet or more tall and provide sturdy support for this vigorous perennial. Leaves are alternate along the stem with petioles sometimes longer than the leaf itself. Leaves may be as much as 6 inches long. Their shapes vary from that of an elongated triangle to having three or five lobes. Three-lobed leaves are common with two short but sharp basal lobes and a longer center lobe, also sharp. This shape resembles that of the halberd, a hand weapon of ancient times. Leaf margins have coarse teeth that are shallow and somewhat rounded.

The flowers are perhaps the most spectacular of our woodlands because of their size and coloring. They have five oval petals, each sometimes more than 3 inches long. The petals are pink to flesh colored with a reddish-purple blotch at the base. Thus, the flower appears to have a much darker center. From this dark center protrudes a long style surrounded by a cylinder of delicate stamens. Each flower has its own short slender stalk arising from the axil of an upper leaf. Surrounding the base of each flower are several green linear bracts to three-fourths inch long. The flowers tend to open briefly about mid-morning and provide one of our woodland's most spectaclar sights.

An inch-long pointed-oval seed capsule with five cells tends to remain on the plant into the winter. Each cell contains several seeds covered with silky hairs – evidence of this plant's family relationship to cotton.

Other species may also be found in the state. Any large pink, white or cream-colored flower with a dark center growing on a large plant brightening a swampy area during late summer is likely to be a species of rose mallow *(Hibiscus).*

No food or medicinal uses of rose mallow by Indians and pioneers are known. But their large size and conspicuous beauty assure that this genus did not go unnoticed. Seeds are eaten by water fowl and sometimes by quail.

Some mallows are locally known as shoe black plants because the petals were once used as a substitute for a polishing cloth to put a mirrow polish on shoes.

The mallow family includes well-known plants such as cotton, hollyhocks, okra, rose of sharon, and several species of hibicus flowers.

. . . photograph by James P. Rowan

Wild lettuce: *Lactuca* many species

Other common names: compass plant, prickly lettuce, wild opium.

Lactuca: from ancient Latin for "milk" referring to the milky juice of the genus.

Species: several blue-flowered and yellow-flowered species are common. Identification is often highly technical. *L. floridana* (L.) Gaertn. is shown.

Daisy family: *Asteraceae (Compositae).*

Found throughout the state under a wide range of environmental conditions. Blooms July to frost.

This genus is widely varied with some species growing as much as 10 feet tall. Rigid erect stems usually have numerous short side-branches, especially toward the top.

Numerous alternate leaves are mostly 4 to 12 inches long and perhaps one-third as wide. The margins are irregularly indented – often resembling the common dandelion leaf. The leaves have a tendency to twist sideways so their surface is vertical.

Some species are hairy. One called prickly lettuce, *L. scariola* L., has weak spines on the leaf margins and stiffer ones on the midrib. The foliage is usually a bright green, sometimes with a whitish bloom. The milky juice is similar to that of the milkweeds.

Ray flowers of the flowerheads are mostly blue to white, sometimes yellow. Individual flowerheads are small, mostly less than a half-inch across, and daisy-like. They are borne in loose open clusters near the top of the plant. Each cluster has relatively few flowers – usually less than a dozen. Upper flowerheads of the clusters bloom first. As they mature, blooming moves progressively lower.

The blue-flowered species are mostly perennials with deep tap roots. Other species may be biennial or annual.

Seeds of this genus are typically small. Their unique feature is their tapering into a beak which is slightly expanded at its tip – as the flare of a trumpet – from which extends a mass of soft hairs.

Tender young shoots of wild lettuce have been used in salads and as a potherb since pre-Christian times. Ancient records indicate use by Romans and by Persian kings as early as 400 B.C. With maturity, however, the plants develop a bitter taste making them less suitable for food use..

The chemical, lactucarium, or lettuce opium, is found to a small degree in most species giving them slight narcotic and sedative properties. In early medicine, wild lettuces were used as a sedative, laxative, and diuretic. Early settlers also used the juice as a nerve tonic.

Both Indians and pioneers used a leaf tea to hasten milk flow after childbirth. The Menomini tribe used the milky juice on poison ivy rash. Chippewas treated warts in the same way. The Meskwaki used the juice for various infantile diseases.

Common garden lettuce, *L. sativa* L., was probably developed from a species also native to Europe, *L. scariola* L.

*. . . photograph by Ray Schulenberg
courtesy of Morton Arboretum*

Goldenrod: *Solidago* many species

Other common names: flower of gold, yellow top, yellow weed.

Solidago: probably from Latin *solidare* meaning "to strengthen or unite", most likely in reference to healing qualities attributed to some species.

Species: many species known in the state are separated by small technical differences in most cases. Species may hybridize producing intermediate types.

Daisy family: *Asteraceae (Compositae).*

Found throughout the state in dry open woods, especially woodland edges, fence rows, and roadsides. Blooms July until frost.

These perennial plants range up to 8 feet tall, mostly less, with slender erect stems. Most stems are unbranched; with a few species, sparsely branched.

Leaves are alternate along the stem and mostly lance-shaped, sometimes to more than 6 inches long and 1½ inch wide. Most are much smaller. Shape also varies from broadly oval to narrow and almost grass-like. Leaves near the base are often smaller than those above and may drop off before flowering. Veining varies from parallel to feather-like.

Leaf margins are usually shallow-toothed with wide variation in size, number, and type of teeth. Leaves are without petioles or mostly so.

Goldenrod plants are perennial, growing from root systems with rhizomes, runners or crowns. As a result, golden rod plants are often found growing in large colonies.

Tiny yellow disc and ray flowers are massed in showy clusters at the top of the stem.

The rays are not numerous – ususally 10 or less. They are quite small so close examination is necessary to appreciate the actual complexity of the individual flowers.

In some species, spikes of flowers are arranged along one side of the stem. In others, the spikes may be on two sides, or all around the stem. In some cases, the flowers are somewhat larger, fewer, and arranged close to the main stem to give a club-like head. In still others, the cluster may be flat-topped.

At least one species has white flowers, and rare albino mutations may occur in species with normally yellow flowers.

Goldenrods are often blamed for hayfever symptoms. But pollination is mostly by insects. Pollen grains may be carried by the wind, but not nearly so much as ragweed pollen.

Both Indians and pioneers used goldenrod for burns, intestinal disorders, and lung problems. They also used leaves of some species as a tea substitute. Other Indian uses included treatment of fevers, bee stings, and diseases of women.

The Meskwaki tribe also burned the plant to produce a smoke inhalant for a person who had fainted. In their early tribal medicine, they also cooked goldenrod with bone of an animal that died about the same time a baby was born, and then washed the baby in the resulting liquid to insure its ability to talk and laugh.

. . . photograph by William Heard

White snakeroot: *Eupatorium rugosum* Houtt.

Other common names: deerwort, poolwort, rich weed, snake weed, squaw weed, white sanicle.

Eupatorium: from Greek meaning generally "good father", in honor of Mithridates Eupator (132-63 B.C.) who is said to have used a species of this genus in medical practice.

Rugosum: from Latin for "wrinkled", probably referring to the appearance of the leaves.

Daisy family: *Asteraceae (Compositae).*

Found widely throughout the state in the partial shade of rich and rocky woodlands, often at the base of bluffs or the edge of clearings. Blooms July to October.

This plant grows erect to 5 feet tall. The stem is much branched near the top. It feels somewhat sticky to the touch. Large leaves, to 6 inches long and 3 inches wide, grow opposite along the stem. They are somewhat heart-shaped with a sharply pointed tip. The network of veins is conspicuous giving the leaf a slightly crinkled appearance. Margins are sharply toothed. Slender petioles vary from a half to 2½ inches long.

The perennial root system is a tough knotty rhizome with extensive fibrous rootlets.

Tight little "buttons" of tiny snowy-white flowers grow pointed upward in loose open flat-topped clusters 2 to 3 inches across. Stalks of the flower clusters arise from the axils of the upper leaves. The bright snowy-whiteness of white snakeroot is so distinctive it helps white snakeroot stand out among other white flowers which bloom in the woodlands during late summer and fall months.

Fruits are small black seeds about one-eight inch long and crowned with a tuft of hairs.

White snakeroot was responsible for "milk sickness" in many parts of the frontier. It probably caused more deaths than any other disease in those times. Cows that eat the plant (usually when no other forage is available) secrete a poison, tremetol, into their milk. The cattle themselves develop a disease, called trembles from its chief symptom. Abraham Lincoln's mother supposedly died of milk sickness.

In early days of frontier settlement, many people in some localities would be affected by the milk and large numbers would die. Not knowing the actual cause, some pioneers believed a curse lay on the land and moved elsewhere. Confusion over the actual cause of the disease continued until the turn of this century.

Pioneers sometimes used white snakeroot to treat urinary disorders. Indians sometimes burned the plant as a smoke inhalant to revive a person who had fainted. The Indian name used by some tribes even translates generally as "smoke a person".

. . . photograph by Alvin F. Bull

Hog peanut: *Amphicarpa bracteata* (L.) Fern.

Other common names: American licorice, peavine, wild peanut.

Amphicarpa: from Greek meaning "two-fruited" referring to two kinds of fruits.

Bracteata: from Latin meaning "bracted", referring to prominent bracts beneath the flower.

Legume family: *Fabaceae (Leguminosae).*

Found throughout the state in moist to wet woodlands, especially along stream banks. Blooms August to September.

The delicate slender stems and branches to 8 feet long are usually covered with reddish-brown hairs. The branching is usually from near the base with few if any branches above. Hog peanut tends to twine over other plants in a tangled mass.

The alternate leaves on long petioles are divided into three leaflets. Each leaflet, to 2 inches long, is rounded at the base and pointed at the tip. Fine stiff hairs are common on both sides of the leaflets. Vegetative characteristics may vary widely from plant to plant.

Flowers of two, sometimes three, kinds are produced by this unusual plant. The above-ground flowers are pea-like, to a half inch long. They vary from purple to mostly pale lilac to white. They grow in drooping clusters of two to 15 flowers on flower stalks arising from leaf axils. The clusters of flowers may also contain a few smaller and incomplete flowers which produce no fruit.

The complete flowers produce a curved pod perhaps an inch and a half long and containing three or four seeds. The pods may be either hairy or smooth.

Creeping thread-like branches of the perennial root system bear self-pollinated flowers which have no petals. These flowers produce a pear-shaped pod with one large fleshy seed or "peanut." Generally, they are found just under the surface of soil that is covered with dead leaves. These somewhat flattened bean-like seeds are usually from one-fourth to one-half inch across.

Both kinds of seeds were used as food by Indians and pioneers. The "peanuts" were sometimes eaten raw. But both kinds of seed were usually roasted or boiled before eating. The leathery skin or shell of the underground fruit cracks off during boiling.

Field mice and other underground rodents often store quantites of seed in their nests for a winter food supply. Indians robbed these caches when they could find them. The Dakota tribes particularly favored leaving an equal amount of grain for the rodents to avoid angering the powers which looked after the welfare of the rodents.

As is typical of members of the legume family, hog peanut has bacteria in its root nodules which take nitrogen from the air for use by the plant. When the vegetative parts decay, much of the nitrogen taken from the air enriches the soil for future plant growth.   *. . . photograph by William Welker*

Closed gentian: *Gentiana andrewsii* Griseb.

Other common names: barrel gentian, blind gentian, bottle gentian, cloistered heart.

Gentiana: named for the ancient King Gentius of Illyria who supposedly discovered the medical properties of some gentians. The gentian he knew was another genus, however.

Andrewsii: honoring Henry C. Andrews, English botanical artist and engraver of the early 19th century.

Gentian family: *Gentianaceae.*

Found throughout the state on rich damp soils of low thickets and woodland edges. Blooms late August to frost.

Stout erect leafy stems, usually without branches, grow to 20 inches tall. The perennial root system is long and coarse.

Leaves are long-oval to lance-shaped, pointed at the tip, and narrowing toward the base. Veining is parallel. Margins tend to be smooth, sometimes irregular with a tiny fringe. Leaves are opposite along the stem and without petioles, or essentially so. Upper leaves are larger than lower ones. Those toward the top may be 4 inches or longer. Uppermost leaves tend to form a whorl of four to six at the base of the main flower head. In late summer a bronze tinge may develop at the leaf tip and along the nearby margin.

Unusual bottle or club-shaped flowers to 2 inches long vary from an intense bright blue or purple to lighter shades and rarely to white. They are closely set, without individual flower stalks, in the axils of upper leaves. Usually, only the uppermost cluster has more than just one or two "bottles." The petals remain essentially closed, joined by a whitish membrane, even when in full bloom. They appear more as a bud about to open. Closed gentian is one of the last of the flowers to bloom in the autumn – sometimes just before the first hard frost of the season.

Authorities disagree about whether or not closed gentian is self fertilized. Only strong and persistent bees, such as the bumble bee, can force entry.

The fruit is a dry upright capsule containing many extremely small seeds.

Both Meskwaki and Potawatomi tribes used the closed gentian as a treatment for snakebite. Women of some tribes ate a piece of closed gentian root for caked breasts. Catawba Indians boiled roots in water and used the resulting liquid to treat backache.

Pioneers ate the root of this species to promote appetite. They also used a tea brewed from the plant to aid digestion – especially following malaria and infectious diseases.

Still later, some Appalachian mountain men carried, or wore around their necks, a piece of the rhizome of a closely related species, *G. villosa* L., in the belief that it increased their physical powers. In Switzerland, a potent alcoholic beverage called Gentiane is fermented from the roots of a related species *(G. lutea* L.) The poorer people of Sweden used *G. campestris* L. in place of hops to brew their ale. ...*photograph by James P. Rowan*

Jerusalem artichoke: *Helianthus tuberosus* L.

Other common names: Canada potato, girasole.

Helianthus: from Greek meaning "sun flower" because flower-heads of this genus are turned with the sun each day.

Tuberosus: from Latin meaning "with tubers."

Daisy family: *Asteraceae (Compositae).*

Found throughout the state on rich soils of open areas and woodland borders. Blooms August through October.

The rough coarse hairy stem, often branched toward the top, grows to 12 feet high. Its thick coarsely-toothed leaves have short petioles and conspicuous veins. They are broadly lance-shaped to 9 inches long and 3 inches wide. Their surfaces are rough and hairy above, downy beneath. Lower leaves are opposite or in whorls of three. Upper leaves are alternate.

The extensive perennial root system produces numerous fleshy tubers.

Loose clusters with few flowerheads on individual stalks occur at tips of the branches. The flowerheads have a small center disc, perhaps a half inch across, surrounded by 10 to 20 conspicuous light yellow rays. Each ray, usually more than an inch long, is notched at its tip.

The common name is believed to be based on misunderstanding of the Italian word "girasole" which means "turning to the sun". Flower buds of some edible sunflowers were boiled and eaten with butter as were artichokes. The combination perhaps resulted in "Jerusalem artichoke."

The potato-like tubers, of irregular shape, have long been an important source of food for Indians who introduced early colonists to this use. The colonists, in turn, exported the plant to Europe where it found great favor until replaced by potatoes. It now grows wild there.

Indians even cultivated the plant. They ate the tubers raw, boiled, or baked. The Chippewas called the plant "askibwan" meaning "raw thing." The Meskwaki name was "sasakihagi."

Explorers Lewis and Clark, in their journal entry April 9, 1805, described how their guide Sacajawea left the party briefly and returned with an abundance of tubers to extend their food supply. These were almost surely the tubers of Jerusalem artichoke.

The tubers when properly prepared may be eaten by diabetics because they contain little sugar and almost no starch. The carbohydrate is in the form of inulin, a major ingredient of diabetic bread. The tubers have also been used as a source material for producing levulose and industrial alcohol.

The tubers are sometimes available in natural food stores. Seed or nursery catalogs frequently offer tubers for planting in home gardens as an interesting substitute for potatoes. They are planted in much the same manner. This is one of the few wild plants which can be harvested without danger of destroying the stand of plants. In his book *Stalking the Wild Asparagus* naturalist Euell Gibbons includes a recipe for artichoke chiffon pie in the section of Jerusalem artichoke.   *...photograph by Lloyd Huff*

Aster: *Aster* many species

Other common names: Mostly aster. Some localized common names such as frostflower or starwort, are used to designate certain species.

Aster: From Greek meaning "star", in reference to the general shape of the flower and its bracts.

Species: At least 200 species are found in North America, many in this state. Differences between species are often minor. Some natural hybridizing also occurs.

Daisy family: *Asteraceae (Compositae).*

Found throughout the state in a wide range of habitats varying from marsh to woodland to prairie. Asters usually grow in colonies, frequently covering large areas. The flowers, often striking in color and appearance, appear from July through frost, mostly late in the season.

Asters generally have stout leafy stems with numerous branches. Among the largest is the New England aster (*A. novae-angliae* L.) which grows 6 or more feet tall. It's showy purple flower heads with conspicuous orange centers may be an inch across.

The white heath aster (*A. pilosus* Willd.), in contrast, grows only to about 3 feet and has flowerheads perhaps a half inch across. Some less common species are typically only a few inches tall.

Leaves of aster plants are alternate and numerous, but vary widely with the species. Some appear as large pointed hearts with toothed margins and long petioles. Still others are toothless and narrow lance shaped which clasp the stem. Other variations are numerous.

Most asters are perennials with substantial branching root systems. A few are annuals or biennials.

Asters have distinctive flowerheads which provide identification of the genus – and sometimes of the species. A single, sometimes double, set of ray flowerlets surround a central disc-shaped cluster of tiny yellow tubular flowerlets. The yellow disc may turn to purple with age. The colorful rays provide some of nature's brightest colors – blue, purple, sometimes shades of red. Numerous flowerheads, one-fourth to 2 inches across depending upon the species, are usually borne in loose heads near the tops of the branches.

The common white heath aster resembles daisy fleabane which flowers earlier in the season. Asters have several circles of bracts around the flowerhead while fleabane has only one.

Leaves of the large-leaf aster, (*A. macrophyllus* L.) have been used as greens when young and fresh. Both Ojibwa and Chippewa Indians used the plant in this manner. Several tribes thought smoke of burning aster plants to be helpful in reviving a person who had fainted. Meskwaki Indians made a smudge from blossoms of *A. lateriflorus* Britt. to treat insanity. They also used the large-leaf aster to treat a mother whose baby was born dead. Some tribes brewed a tea of aster plants for headache. Some species even served as a charm.

. . . photograph by Donald R. Kurz

Scouring rush: *Equisetum* several species

Other common names: bottle brush, cat's tail, horsetail rush, jointgrass, snakegrass, snakepiper, snake weed, toadpipe.

Equisetum: from Latin *equus* for "horse" and *seta* for "bristle."

Species: Most common are *E. arvense* L. (of cultivated fields) and *E. hyemale* L. (of winter – because of its evergreen character). Other species are also found in the state.

Horsetail family: *Equisetaceae.*

Found throughout the state in wet woodlands and sometimes in open areas. This genus produces no flowers.

Erect arrow-like stems are hollow and jointed. Various species grow from a few inches to 5 feet in height. Stems of *E. arvense* are of two types. The early ones are tan or brown and terminate in a cone-like spike about an inch long which produces the reproductive spores. These weak stems grow to about 10 inches tall and die back in early spring. They are followed by pale green stems to 2 feet tall. Slender green branches arise in whorls from the nodes. Further branching may occur on the branches.

The unbranched green stems of *E. hyemale* L. are distinctly ridged and rough to touch. They grow to about 3 feet tall. Conical heads produce reproductive spores.

In this genus leaves are vestigial (no longer functional), reduced to scales which join in whorls at the joints forming a papery sheath around the stem. The green stems, instead of leaves, perform photosynthesis for the plant. The roots are horizontal perennial rhizomes which are jointed in much the same manner as the stems.

Young shoots of some *Equisetum* species have been used for food as far back as ancient Rome. *E. pratense* Ehrh. produces tubers which were eaten by Indians of Minnesota.

Potawatomi Indians fed *E. arvense* L. to captive wild geese and expected it to make them fat within a week. The Meskwaki tribe fed *E. hyemale* L. to their ponies for the same purpose.

Later, squaws of both tribes used the plants to scour pots and pans – as did early pioneers. Silica is imbedded in the cell walls providing a gritty material for polishing. Western Indians even used it to put the final sharp edge on arrowheads.

Some Indian tribes, especially those of the west, also found medical uses for these plants. They made a tea of the plant to treat kidney troubles and dropsy. Reproductive heads were eaten for diarrhea.

A Washington tribe even boiled the plant in water to make a shampoo for getting rid of lice and mites.

Our present *Equisetum* species are what remain of an ancient genus of prehistoric times. Fossils of species which grew as much as 90 feet tall and one foot in diameter have been found in coal beds.

Several species, mainly *E. arvense* L. have been reported as poisonous to horses. Apparently, eating large amounts causes a thiamine deficiency.   *...photograph by Kitty Kohout*

INDEX